THE FABULOUS

MOOLAH

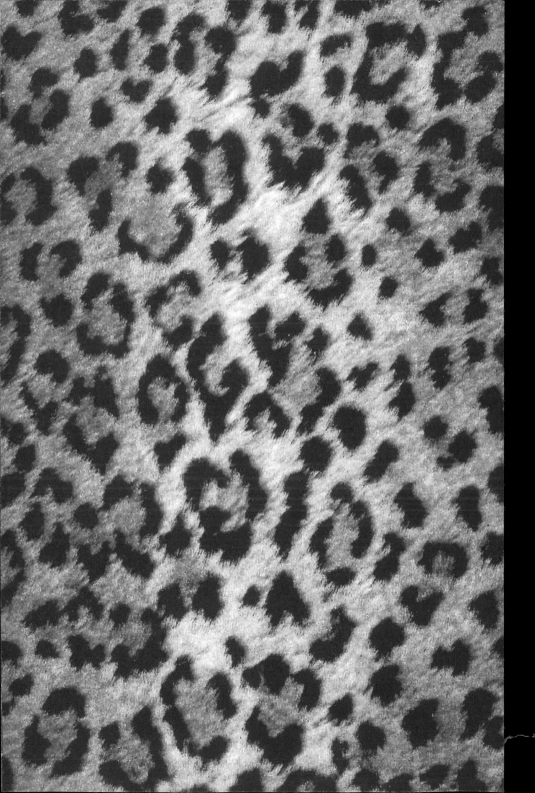

THE FABULOUS MOOLAH

FIRST GODDESS OF THE SQUARED CIRCLE

LILLIAN ELLISON

with Larry Platt

ReganBooks
An Imprint of HarperCollinsPublishers

Photographs on pages 1, 7, 25, 34, 39, 44, 53, 58, 61, 62, 93, 99, 172, 207, 217, and 221 courtesy of Lillian Ellison.

Photographs on pages iii, vi, 15, 20, 71, 79, 87, 103, 113, 120, 125, 131, 136, 141, 144, 151, 157, 167, 179, 187, 193, 201, 213, 224, and 227 courtesy of Pro Wrestling Illustrated.

Photograph on page 199 courtesy of World Wrestling Entertainment.

HarperCollins books may be purchased for educational, business, or sales promotional use. For information please write: Special Markets Department, HarperCollins Publishers Inc., 10 East 53rd Street, New York, NY 10022.

FIRST EDITION

Designed by Joel Avirom and Jason Snyder
Design Assistant: Meghan Day Healey

Printed on acid-free paper

Library of Congress Cataloging-in-Publication Data
Ellison, Lillian.
    The Fabulous Moolah: first goddess of the squared circle/Lillian Ellison.—1st ed.
    p. cm.
    ISBN 0-06-039397-1
    1. Ellison, Lillian. 2. Women wrestlers—United States—Biography. 3. Wrestlers—United States—Biography. I. Title.
GV1196.E56 A3 2002
796.812'092—dc21
[B]
2002017852

02 03 04 05 06 ❖/RRD 10 9 8 7 6 5 4 3 2 1

This book is dedicated to all of my fans
and to the wonderful McMahon family—
most especially Vince Sr.

CONTENTS

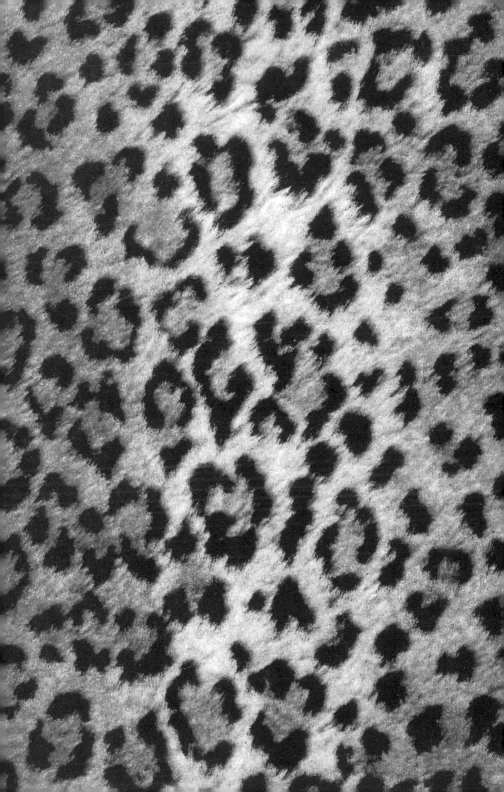

1

AN ASS-KICKING GREAT-GRANDMA

I DON'T MIND TELLING YA, DARLIN', it got me revved up. It always did. Any crowd noise, cheers or catcalls. Used to be, the crowd would always cheer for whoever I was going against. That was okay; I loved for the fans to hate me. It made me put on a better show. *I'll show you*, I'd say to myself when I'd hear them call me "Bitch!" or "SOB!"—two of my favorite, uh, nicknames.

But now they were cheering *for* me, and I was as revved up as in the old days. It was 1999 and we were in Cleveland when Ivory, the World Wrestling Entertainment's Undisputed Women's Champion, came stomping down the runway toward me in the ring. I was wearing my multicolored sequined jacket over my green leotard, my hair and makeup had been done that morning, and I was looking like a lady should look—even a lady about to kick the butt of someone young enough to be her granddaughter. The folks in the arena and those watching at home may have been on my side

because they thought I was some kind of novelty act, standing there in my seventies, about to lock horns with the top lady wrestler in the country. That's what Jerry Lawler, one of the TV announcers, thought. I like Jerry, even though I have to give him a piece of my mind now and again when he starts ripping on women's wrestling. "Can you imagine losing your championship to a senior citizen like that?" Jerry said on national TV when the camera focused on me in the ring. "The only thing worse than that would be losing your virginity to one!" That's real funny, but it also goes to show that Jerry, like most people, wasn't really serious about what was about to happen. I was dead serious, especially since I got all revved up when I first saw Ivory make her entrance.

See, she came into the ring that night showing off my property. Wouldn't you scratch and claw and kick and yank hair for something that was rightfully yours? That's exactly what I was thinking. *She's got something that's mine. And she's waving it around like it's hers.* Around her right shoulder, see, was a World Wrestling Entertainment Undisputed Women's Championship belt. Not just any championship. *The Championship.* The championship belt that had spent twenty-eight years around my waist, from the time I won it in 1956 until Wendi Richter took it from me in 1984, because a damned ref counted me down when I not only had *my* shoulder off the mat, but I had a pin hold on Wendi, too. Of course the next year, I got *my championship* back from Wendi—who, like so many other girls, I had trained—and

that's where it's stayed, right around my waist, for the next two years. Let me put this in perspective for you: When I first won the championship in 1956, Hulk Hogan was two years old, Dwight D. Eisenhower was president, and I *Love Lucy* was the top show on TV. When I lost the championship to Wendi, Ronald Reagan was president and Madonna was the top singer. I always let my actions in the ring speak for me, and I don't like to sound like I'm bragging, but think about it: You read today about athletes who dominate, about the Tiger Woodses and Michael Jordans, but there is only one sports figure to my mind who was at the top of her game for thirty out of thirty-one years and who then came back twelve years later, in 1999, to challenge for the championship for a third time.

That's right, I'm talking about that great-grandma in the ring that night in Cleveland, yours truly. I'll never forget the way Ivory sashayed her way into the squared circle, waving that championship belt. My partner in crime, Mae Young, was by my side. You'll hear lots of stories about crazy ol' Mae in the pages ahead—she's even older than me, but she can still kick ass and take names. Mae was the main reason I was even there, in that ring, challenging for the championship. Like I said, it's not like me to go around telling folks how great I am, but Mae has always been an in-your-face talker. Well, backstage at one World Wrestling Entertainment show, Mae was feelin' no pain and she got right up in the champ's face and boomed: "You ain't never really had an ass-whuppin' till

you got it from Moolah!" The gauntlet was thrown, and the next thing you knew, there we were, Mae and me, a couple of senior citizens, watching Ivory approach as the fans cheered.

Mae, who was standing just outside the ropes, looked sad as she eyed the champ up and down. "Poor girl," she said. "She don't know what's coming."

"You can say that again," I said.

"Poor girl. She don't know what's coming."

Just then, Ivory jumped into the ring and made another mistake. She opened her big mouth. "You got it comin', and you're gonna get it from a real champ tonight!" she screamed at me, babbling like a catfish: all mouth and no brains.

"We'll just see," I said, staring her down coldly.

Turns out, Ivory is a pretty good wrestler, for what she knows. The bell rang and she came charging, sending me reeling into the ropes with a flying dropkick. I was still dazed a moment later, flat on my back, with Ivory covering me and the ref pounding the canvas. That's when a lifetime of wrestling instinct kicked in. No way was I about to be pinned less than a minute into a championship match. Without really thinking about it, I kicked out, surprising Ivory, who must have already been preparing her postmatch line of bullcrap. Next thing you knew, there we were, toe-to-toe, and Ivory seemed stunned when I followed up a couple of open hand slaps to the face by grabbing a good fistful of her hair—there's nothing

THE FABULOUS MOOLAH

5

like a good fistful of hair in the ring. And now this great-grandma was flipping her to and fro across the ring. She knew darn well she was in a battle.

As the war waged on I knew that Mae would be circling the ring, looking for an opening. Once, when I had Ivory up against the ropes, Mae came up from behind and kicked at her and Ivory turned around and—*boom!*—dropped Mae with a right hand that had the crowd buzzing. But that got me thinking. If Mae could shake off the cobwebs, the next time she distracted Ivory, I could move in for the kill.

Minutes later, the chance came. I gotta hand it to Ivory, she wasn't interested in just beating me, she wanted to beat me with the very championship belt that had belonged to me for so long. That's something I would have done, too, 'cause I didn't just want to win—I wanted to humiliate my opponent in the ring and then walk off smiling like the demure Southern belle I really am. So Ivory grabbed the championship belt and stood over me, about to crash it down on my head. That would have been it for Moolah.

But Ivory didn't count on Mae reaching from behind and grabbing a clump of that beautiful hair. Enraged, Ivory wheeled around and—*boom!*—the championship belt came crashing down on Mae, who again went flying. That's Mae for you. Even when she's not on the card, she's liable to get the crap kicked out of her and keep coming back for more. As soon as Ivory turned, I knew I had to move

quickly. I grabbed her around the hips and rolled her up so she landed on her back, with me covering her. The ref slammed the canvas three times; the bell rang; and the championship belt that had just bopped Mae over that granite head of hers was handed back to me. It felt right, like a baby being returned to its mama. Ivory jumped up, tears streaming down her face, and you could barely hear the announcer over the roar of the crowd: "Ladies and gentlemen! The winner and new Women's Champion, the Fabulous Moolah!"

I looked at Mae, and she at me, as we were crushed by well-wishers on our way to the dressing room. I kept thinking, *I'm the champ again—in my seventies!* I thought of all the wacky characters I knew and loved and battled during a lifetime in this crazy business, and a lump formed in my throat. I'd just done something nobody had ever done. *I'm the champ again—in my seventies!* At moments like these, Mae is the perfect sidekick, because there's no room for sentiment where Mae Young is concerned. She just looked right at me as the welts started to form on top of her head and said, "Boy, do I need a drink."

✦   ✦   ✦

"Moolah! Where you been?!"

That's what so many fans screamed at me during my comeback run in 1999. They were the ones who remembered me from days gone by; there were plenty more who had started following World Wrestling Entertainment in the nineties, so I pretty much jumped straight out of the record book to give them a glimpse of history-in-the-making once I came back. I had kept a low profile in the nineties, teaching girls to wrestle at my school in Columbia, South Carolina, and enjoying my days on my Columbia estate—located

on Moolah Drive. I'm sitting here right now, on my big, old country porch, right on the water, where it's very peaceful and calm. Katie, my damned midget, has been with me forty years, ever since she was seventeen years old and sought me out because she dreamed of becoming a wrestler. You might know her better as the midget wrestler Diamond Lil. But in 1999, I introduced her to the nation as "my damned midget" on *The Daily Show* with Jon Stewart, and that's what I've called her ever since. She calls me Ma, and I guess I've been a sort of mother figure to her.

Mae has lived here with us for about ten years now. She had quit wrestling and moved out to California to become an evangelist—as if she could make up for all her earlier hell-raising—and to care for her mother. Well, her mother passed and so did her sister and brother. So Mae was out there all alone in 1991 when Katie and I went to visit.

"Mae," I said. "Come on back with me and Katie. Live with us back in Columbia. At least you won't be alone."

She had already had about enough of that evangelical racket and figured there wasn't really anything keeping her out there on the West Coast. So she moved in with us, and it's been a barrel of laughs ever since. Sometimes Mae doesn't see too good, so I like to play tricks on her. For example, I got me a life-size cardboard cutout of Stone Cold Steve Austin and put it smack-dab in the center of our living room. Well, Mae came trudging on down the stairs

THE FABULOUS MOOLAH

9

and I called out to her, "Mae, this gentleman wants us to teach him how to wrestle!" Don't you know she walked right up to Stone Cold, stuck out her hand, and said, "How do you do? So you wanna wrestle?" Only when he didn't make a move to shake her hand did she inch closer and squint at him and jump back with a start, thinking at first that it really was Stone Cold, then realizing, when she heard my giggling, that it was only cardboard.

We sure do have us some fun. This is where we were when Vince McMahon called me in late 1998 and invited me to make the unprecedented comeback that culminated in my pinning Ivory that night. I soon learned how much pro wrestling had changed. It was big business now—show business. The first check we got, Mae stared at it for several minutes. "That's thousands, not hundreds," I told her. She didn't believe me at first, so I offered to take the check and handle her money for her, but she was smart enough to see through that old trick.

When Vince called, I eagerly took him up on his offer. First of all, I knew that I could still rock-and-roll inside the squared circle. I've got a wrestling ring at home, which is where I teach all my girls, and where Mae, Katie, and I go every now and again to knock each other around. But I also wanted to come back to prove a point to people my age. Life doesn't have to end when you get that AARP card in the mail. Mae, Katie, and I stay away from senior citizens' outings, because it always feels like too many people our age give

in, give up, and stop living. I've always been about getting off of my ass and going after life, rather than waiting around to die. I figured if, by watching me, one sixty- or seventy-something fan gets up off his or her duff and goes out and does something, experiences something new, different, and challenging, well, then my comeback will be well worth it.

That's also the way I feel about my story. See, from the get-go, I did things my way. When I was coming up, it was unheard of for a lady wrestler to be strong and independent. We were the valets for the men stars, and we had men—promoters, other wrestlers, husbands, or boyfriends—telling us exactly what to do. Well, I never did listen to any of them. I did what I wanted to do, ever since I was a little girl and defied my dear daddy's wishes by entering the ring.

Now don't get me wrong: I love men. I should—I married my share of them. And that doesn't count my romance with country star Hank Williams Sr., who asked me to marry him. Yeah, I love men, but I can't stand being controlled by them. From the earliest age, I knew I owed it to myself to do whatever I wanted; if I made mistakes, well, at least they'd be *my* mistakes.

I know I sound all tough and daring, but it's not really like that, not all the time. There are really two people talking to you here: the wild and crazy Moolah, who will defy anything and everyone, who will ignore the rules if it means winning, who will bask in the boos from the crowd; but there's also the Southern belle Lillian Ellison, who is a great-grandma, who calls everyone darlin', and who every week calls her great-grandchildren—the apples of my eye—to hear the five-year-old twins say, "Do you smell what The Rock is cookin'?" in a singsong voice that makes me want to giggle and cry at the same time. For the past fifty years, people who have met me outside the ring have said how shocked they were by how much of a lady I am, how I'm not a bitch. Well, in this book you're going to get both: the kindly great-grandma who never has a bad word to say about anyone—that is, until—as Katie always points out—someone crosses me. That's when the Moolah personality comes out, and you've seen what kind of damage she can do.

You'll meet them both, and you'll get a couple of surprises, too. See, I don't think it's ladylike to give out my age, but I might just break that rule by telling you at the very end of this book how old Moolah really is. And I'll let you in on a little secret I've been entertaining: My 1999 comeback might not have been my last. I've gone through medical hell the past two years, but now I've emerged stronger, healthier, and more confident in God's plan for me. So listen to what Moolah's telling you, because I've been doubted before. If my doctors give me the go-ahead, I just may come on back again. Wouldn't that be something, especially if I make my return against someone like The Rock? That will be the comeback of all comebacks. I don't know if it will happen, but I have a way of turning my dreams into reality. People—even Mae—look at me like I'm

crazy when I start to fantasize about my comeback plans. But they don't realize what I've been through these past two years. Getting in the ring again . . . Hell, that will be easy compared to what I've gone through. After all, between Thanksgiving and Christmas 2000, I literally *died* twice. Now I'm here to tell you that after all that, do you really think anything can stand in Moolah's way?

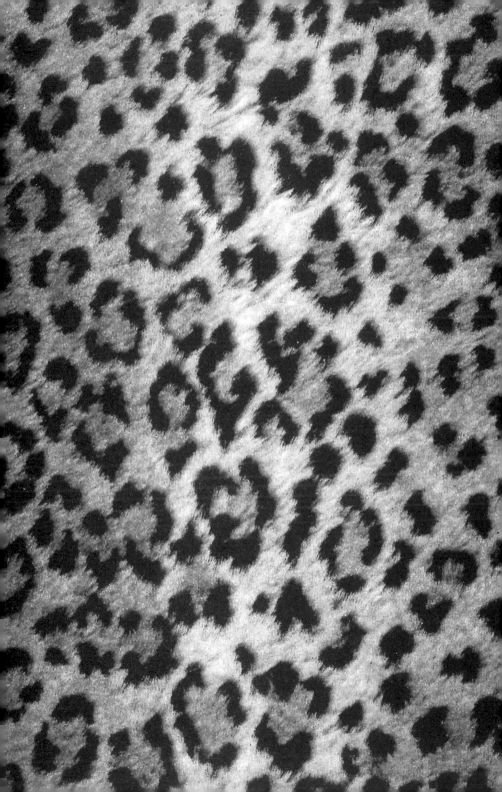

2

DEAD WOMAN WALKING

THEY SAY THAT PAIN IS JUST WEAKNESS leaving the body, and if that's the case, I've let go of more than my share of weakness. There was that time in Toronto when my collarbone shattered and the bone came right up through the skin. I had to wrestle the following night at Madison Square Garden, so I found me a doctor who would just jam that bone right back into place. Course, the pain caused me to pass out, but I was able to make it to the Big Apple.

Then there was the time I broke my neck in Ohio, when The Lady Angel pulled me over the top rope and my head went straight into the mat. I've broken an ankle, torn my rotator cuff, and had my knee knocked out of joint on an almost weekly basis. I reckon I've done something—a break, fracture, sprain, or a twist—to every bone in my body.

Still, I wouldn't change a thing. That is, until I came upon my

Lillian Ellison

toughest fight. Just before Thanksgiving 2000, Moolah almost went down for the count.

All during the time I was wrestling in 1999, I kept a secret from just about everyone—even my beloved daughter, Mary, who lives in Myrtle Beach. At the beginning of that year, I started having dizzy spells. I'd have to steady myself by holding on to a chair, and I felt like I was being spun around at a hundred miles per hour. Must be vertigo, I figured. In April, I started having blackouts. At first I'd hear a pounding—*bum, bum, bum*—in my head, and then I'd start spinning, and I'd yell, "Oh God, stop me!" while the noise in my head got louder and louder, like a freight train, until I'd drop. One night I busted open my head on the radiator in a hotel in Connecticut.

All I kept thinking was *Good God, don't let me pass out in the ring.* Amazingly, it never came on me when I was wrestling. It was as if the only time I was healthy was when I was putting on a good show for the people who booed me or chanted my name. I knew I should tell somebody about what I was going through, but I was just having so much damned fun being back in the World Wrestling Entertainment limelight. My daughter, Mary, could see how much my newfound fame meant to me. She even sent the sweetest note to Vince McMahon, telling him how much I was enjoying myself.

And Mary was right; I was riding high. I had that same feeling I've always gotten when driving the open road behind the wheel of

THE FABULOUS MOOLAH

one of my cars. I recently put a modified motor into my '67 Ford truck that'll get it up to 160 miles per hour—not that I'd ever push it *quite* that high. I'm getting that one done up in candy-apple red with silver spots on it: a Hot Rod Ford. I also got me a Dodge van, a '91 Cadillac, and two '78 Cadillacs. One has 430,000 miles on it. I like to push the pedal to the metal and feel the wind whipping through my hair. That's freedom, and it makes me ecstatic, the same feeling I get inside the squared circle, where my every move sparks a reaction from a packed crowd.

That's the same feeling I was having being back in the ring in 1999. I knew there was something wrong with me, but I didn't tell anyone for fear that I'd be jeopardizing the continuation of my comeback, sacrificing the feeling Mary knew I was basking in. Privately, I started seeing some doctors, nine in all. To a man—and they were all men—they told me that what I was experiencing goes with age, and that I'd have to live with it.

"Bullshit," I said. "My brother Chip is eighty-eight, and he don't have to live with it. Something is wrong."

They did MRIs of my head; they did an ultrasound of my neck to make sure my arteries were open. Nothing showed up.

One day, on a whim, I decided to return a phone call from Dr. Tim Pansegrau. A year earlier, Dr. Tim had treated my darling and closest brother, Bill, for his heart problem. Dr. Tim is the sweetest doctor in the whole world, and he did everything he could. Bill's

heart was still good at the end, but after four months in intensive care, everything else went—the kidneys, lungs, and liver.

Dr. Tim and I cried over Bill's death and started a real friendship. While I was going through my dizzy spells, however, I hadn't returned a number of his calls. When I finally did, he knew something was wrong.

"Lil, you sound depressed," he said.

"I guess that's because it's been a year since Bill died," I said.

Dr. Tim shared my sadness over Bill's loss, and invited me up to the hospital to see him.

"How you been?" he asked over coffee.

"Not worth a damn. I'm afraid to death to drive my car," I blurted out, going on to tell him of my vertigo episodes.

"Have you had your heart checked?" he asked.

"Oh, Tim, there's nothing wrong with my heart," I said. "I can wrestle an hour and I'm not short-winded or tired."

He insisted on checking out my heart and wouldn't take no for an answer. I'm ashamed now to say what I thought: *All along, I thought he was my friend, but here he is, trying to get my money.* Well, turns out that he saved my life. A couple of days after I started wearing a heart monitor, I got a call that they wanted me in the hospital—immediately.

That's when the nightmare started. First they put a couple of needles in me, trying to regulate my heart down to a normal rate.

THE FABULOUS MOOLAH

"Don't move, you've got three needles in your heart," I remember a nurse saying to me as she pumped me full of morphine while a doctor looked at my heart on a computer screen. For two days, they performed exploratory surgery, and I had to keep my legs absolutely straight so my blood wouldn't clot. They found that I had two and a half clogged arteries. But when I finally woke, I was surrounded by a team of doctors. "We can't operate on you," they told me, looking all grave. Turns out I also had a life-threatening case of viral pneumonia.

For the next twenty-four days, I stayed in intensive care, fading in and out. I blacked out through one whole stretch of fifteen days. To this day, I can't remember any more than the fuzzy, dreamy vision I had on the two occasions my heart actually stopped. I was looking down on my lifeless body on that hospital bed. I was a goner for sure.

Every day I was in that hospital, Dr. Tim would come to see me, bless his heart. I remember how, after being out of it for fifteen straight days, I woke up and insisted on trying to walk.

"Are you sure you want to walk?" the nurse asked, looking at me like I was crazy.

"Yes, I'm sure," I said, slowly getting to my feet. "Get me a chair."

She handed me a chair, and I used it like a walker and off I went. Rounding the nurses' station, I saw Dr. Tim with his back to me, standing outside my room. I snuck up on him and threw my arms around him from behind. He spun around and his eyes just about popped out of his head. "Lillian!" he shrieked. "I never thought I'd see you up and around again!"

"It's me, Doc," I said. "Just call me Dead Woman Walking!"

Somehow, I came back. But two days after they released me from the hospital, I blacked out while making my way to the bathroom. I fell on a table; my damned midget Katie heard the crash and came running. She got me off the floor and I was screaming; my back was in agony. I had crushed a few vertebrae. In the ring, I know how to take a bump and land in a way that makes it feel like nothing. But I'm conscious in the ring. Once I blacked out, I didn't stand a chance of cushioning the blow.

By the week of Christmas, crushed vertebrae and all (I never took so many painkillers!), I was strong enough for them to go ahead and successfully perform angioplasty on me. Two months later, it was back to the hospital for a new type of back surgery, where they do it just like they did my heart, putting a needle with a balloon in there and shooting in cement to reconstruct the vertebrae. Now I got cement in my back, so I can crush two or three tables at a time.

Gradually I've built my strength back up. I've even started taking some bumps in the ring. After everything I've been through, I'm convinced there is a reason I'm still here. Now, I'm not one of these

God squadders, you know? I'm a Christian person, and I try to treat everyone the way I want to be treated. But I don't try and push my beliefs on anyone else.

I think my good friend Jesse Ventura was right when he told *Playboy* magazine that religion can be a crutch that weak people lean on. A few years ago, we—the Ladies' International Wrestling Association, which I founded—were going to have a gala during our convention in Las Vegas. I called one of the old-time lady wrestlers to invite her. She said to me, "Let me have a talk with Jesus, and I'll let you know if I can come."

"Well, talk fast and talk hard, because we want you there," I said.

She wrote me a letter, saying she had her little talk with Jesus and he told her she could come to "Sin City." This is what I'm talking about, and I think it's what Jesse was getting at: It's not the religion that's stupid, it's some of the people. I said, "Savannah, Georgia, can be Sin City if you let it. What you do is not what the city tells you to do."

Maybe Jesus called her back and told her not to come, because she never showed up.

That's just what Jesse was talking about: It takes an idiot to act like that. I've seen people just go crazy in taking religion the wrong way. But that doesn't mean I don't believe in Jesus. It just means I don't believe in what some wackos believe *about* Jesus.

THE FABULOUS MOOLAH

23

My damn midget Katie and I talk about this all the time. We talk about how God brought me back for a reason and about how I've got unfinished business. Getting in the ring again—maybe tag-teaming with Stone Cold against The Rock and Mae Young!—is part of it, I think. But I also sense that my unfinished business includes the telling of this story, because if I kick off, an eyewitness to over a half century of wrestling goes with me. And I ain't leaving till I have my say.

3

THE GIRL FROM TOOKIEDOO

IT'S OKAY, SISTER. GET ON IN." That's what my brothers would tell me, giggling all the while, before putting me in a tire on top of a steep hill and pushing me down the hill right into a creek. I was all of five years old, and I loved it. I even pretended to fall for their tricks time and again, because I so loved to show off my toughness.

I was the youngest of thirteen kids—and the only girl. We grew up in the tiny country town of Tookiedoo, South Carolina, about twelve miles outside of Columbia. Calling Tookiedoo a town is being generous, seeing as how we pretty much made up the whole place ourselves. Which made me "The Girl from Tookiedoo." My ma and pa had a farm, a grocery store, and a service station. Daddy had a sawmill, and he and my mom cut all the lumber they used to build our home. They were quite a pair. Daddy was half Cherokee Indian, and Mama was full Irish.

Lillian Ellison

Growing up surrounded by twelve boys, I had to be tough from the get-go. At five years older, Bill was the brother closest to me in age, so he was often my partner in crime. I do so miss him, today and every day. We used to get mad at the other boys. They'd take the horses out without letting us ride, so we'd find rocks about the size of an egg and we'd hide behind the house, and when they'd come back, we'd start firing the rocks at them—a surprise-attack rock war.

Ours was the first family we knew who had electric lights. My dad got us a generator and that was a big deal in the county. Our cousins from Camden, South Carolina, about thirty miles away, would come down every Sunday for dinner. After dinner, we'd play "pop the whip," turning that generator into a party toy. What we'd do is all hold hands in a line, and the one that we wanted to get popped, we'd put on the end of the line, farthest from the generator. While holding hands, we'd all go running and Bill, at the front of the line, would grab the wire on the generator, and the spark of electricity would travel the whole line, picking up in intensity as it went through each person. Whoever was on the end of the line bore the brunt of the shock. Boy, it would knock you right down. We all laughed at whoever got popped, but I have to say that Bill always protected me from being in that position. He always saw to it that I was close to him and the generator's wire, where you'd hardly feel the electric current buzzing through you.

Bill and I used to go fishing almost every day in the creek right near our house. Once, a storm came and blew this big tree across the creek. I must have been about six years old, but already I was showing signs of having no fear. Though Bill knew I was afraid of lizards and snakes. Anyway, Bill wanted me to crawl across the tree and get us more bait.

"Crawl now, don't walk," he called to me. He wanted me to crawl because he didn't want me falling in. That creek was littered with what we called "suck holes"—a whirlpool-like action in the water that sucks anything down that gets near it. Bill didn't know it, and neither did I, but one of those pockets of swirling suction was taking place right near me. Suddenly I came face-to-face with a big, ugly lizard. "Bill! A lizard! I'm gonna jump!" I cried out.

"Sister! Don't jump!" Bill called. "He ain't gonna bother you none."

"If he comes at me, I'm jumping!"

Just then, that ugly old lizard looked right up at me, thrust out his nasty tongue, blinked his beady little eyes, and spat, "Bleeeahhh!" My heart dropped into my stomach. I jumped right off that tree into the water and knew instantly that something was wrong. It felt like my feet were being sucked into a hole. I started screaming—I probably scared that poor lizard!—and clutched for dear life onto nearby berry briars. Bill ran across that tree and grabbed me by the hair as I was about to go under. He yanked at me for what felt like minutes

before his strength started to overcome the power of the suction tugging at my feet. I was crying; he was crying. He held me in his arms and walked all the way back home with me, leaving the fishing poles and bait where they were. "Sister, we're not going fishin' anymore," he told me.

Bill would protect me, but that didn't keep me from mixing it up with the boys. Later, at school, I never shied away from putting a boy bully in his place, in full view of every kid in the school yard. To me, all them boys at school were sissies compared to the battles I'd have to wage at home. Sometimes, Bill and I would take on a couple of our older, bigger brothers in knock-down-drag-out fights where anything—rocks, sticks, kicking, clawing—would go. Looking back on it, those were my first tag-team matches, and probably schooled me in my "anything goes" mentality in the ring. That's why I don't hesitate to pull hair, bite, or sneak-attack in the ring, 'cause if you played fair in my backyard, you ended up in tears.

I was tough, but I was also my mama's little girl. I was the only girl and I was the baby of the family, so Mama had a special place in her heart for me. I was with her all the time. I'd sleep with her and learn from her about hard work. She was tough, too—you don't give birth to thirteen kids by the age of thirty-two, help your husband build your own house, and make your own maple syrup from scratch without having an iron will and fighting spirit.

But there were some things a small-town country woman didn't have the strength to fight in the 1920s. One of them was cancer. My mama died at the age of forty. Now, they say it was cancer, and I'm sure it was. But a part of me has always thought she died from having too many kids, too fast. Her body just gave out. To this day, I don't like talking about losing my mama, because I get all gloomy, and I do my best to stay positive and look to the future. But that hit me hard, I'll tell ya. As I got older, I began to realize that my mama never really left me, that she's always been right here with me in spirit, and that feels good, knowing she is watching her little girl kick butt in the ring, make history, and become famous.

But don't kid yourself, darlin'. No matter how tough a mask she puts on, it is mighty hard on a little girl of eight to lose her mama—especially when she's surrounded by so many boys! I went to live with my grandmom, my daddy's mom. Even though I was so young, I didn't want to depend on my daddy for everything. I think I'm just naturally independent, and like I said, I started that with the girl wrestlers. Before I came along, the girls had no power.

Anyhow, my grandma lived about half a mile from my cousin, who had a big cotton farm. I talked to him and asked if I could pick cotton for him and make me some money during the summer. I didn't want to be asking my daddy for money all the time, like my brothers were doing. Well, my cousin said yes, that he'd pay me *one dollar* for every *one hundred pounds* of cotton I picked. He must

have thought he wouldn't end up having to pay this little eight-year-old girl one red cent.

I'll show him, I thought. Every morning, I'd get up real early and walk the half mile uphill to my cousin's house. There, I'd get two heavy cotton bags; I'd put one sack on each shoulder and make my way to the cotton field. It was early enough in the day when I got there that it wouldn't be too hot out. But since it was so early, the dew was still on the cotton, which made it heavier to pick. Every day, I'd pick and pick, until I had over a hundred pounds—a dollar a day. With that money, I bought my clothes, school supplies, and anything else I needed. This way, I didn't have to be dependent upon my daddy. He said he thought all this work was good for me, but he still slipped me a dollar or two here and there.

My daddy knew that I was a sad little girl who was missing her mama. I was still a tomboy, but I also kind of retreated into my own little shell. I used to fantasize about living another kind of life. I became fascinated by Amelia Earhart and the idea of being an aviator. Could there be anything that made you feel more free than to be charging around up in the air, looking down at all the people locked on the land? Come to think of it, I never gave up my interest in that feeling of ultimate freedom. It's what I get from cruising around on the open road in one of my Caddies. Only difference is that, on the highway, I've always got to keep one eye out for Smokey when my foot becomes a bit heavy on that gas pedal.

THE FABULOUS MOOLAH

Because I was so tough on the outside, it was easy for my brothers and the kids at school—many of whom sported shiners courtesy of yours truly—to forget that I was still a little girl who had lost her mama. But bless his soul, my daddy saw me for who I was. And he saw what I was going through. So he tried to come up with things for just the two of us to do, ways for me to spend special time with him and preoccupy my mind. He was a wrestling fan like you wouldn't believe; he loved it. So one of the things he did was get us ringside seats every Tuesday night for pro wrestling in Columbia. I was ten at the time. At first, I was just excited to be sharing something special with my daddy, without all my brothers hovering around, pulling at my hair, taking potshots at me, and competing for Daddy's attention.

Usually, we watched this big old Indian guy wrestle. I liked it well enough, and Daddy loved it. I'd come home and try out the moves I'd seen on my brothers, some of whom were kind of jealous that I got to go to the fights every week. It was fun and it was something to look forward to. But my Tuesday nights with my daddy at the fights soon came to mean much more to me.

It all changed the night Mildred Burke came to town. She was the Women's Champ at the time. I was a little pipsqueak in pigtails sitting ringside, so I didn't know how things would turn out, that Burke would be followed by June Byers as champ, who would be followed by none other than little old me. But I knew none of that then. All I knew was here was a woman walking into the ring and

Lillian Ellison

every eye in the place was on her. She carried herself the way a champion should. She strutted. I could just tell that here was someone—a lady—who kicked ass and took names. After all this time I had spent surrounded by and competing with boys, here was a woman like Amelia Earhart who I could model myself after.

Mildred Burke wasn't just any champ, by the way. She was *the* champ. She dominated ladies' wrestling. Why, in the 1930s, she even toured the country, challenging men to wrestle her. She took on more than two hundred men and lost only once.

Later on, after I turned professional, I got the chance to meet Mildred Burke, and that was a disappointing experience. I was on my way to a match in Montana and stopped in Omaha, Nebraska, to see her wrestle and to meet her in the dressing room. I was thrilled to meet her, until I actually came face-to-face with her. She was full of herself, reminding everybody that "I'm the champ" over and over again. If there's one thing I can't stand, it's when people who are doing well at the moment treat others below them badly and act like they're God's gift to the universe. So I thought to myself, *You might be the champ, but maybe I'll get a chance someday.* I left that brief meeting thinking that I'd like to take a shot at her right now. I'd have probably gotten the hell beat out of me, because I didn't know nearly enough then, but I was ready to try. I never did get the chance to square off against Mildred Burke, however, because her husband and manager, Billy Wolfe, the scourge of wrestling at the time—

who you'll be hearing lots about in the pages ahead—only let her wrestle girls who he wanted her to wrestle.

'Course, I knew none of this that night my daddy took me to see Mildred Burke put on a show in Columbia. When she came into the ring, my eyes widened and I jumped to my feet. "Wow!" I shouted. "I didn't know girls could do this! I didn't know they did this!"

"Yeah, they do it just like the men," my daddy said.

"I want to wrestle!" I declared. At that moment I could feel my dream of becoming an aviator fly away.

My daddy looked at me with a sideways smile. "Yeah, I know," he said. "You want to do everything."

I don't think he believed me, that this was something I had to do. He didn't want me wrestling. Even as the years passed and it became clear that my obsession wasn't just some passing fancy, he didn't think I belonged there. I think he didn't want me to get hurt, but he always said it wasn't ladylike. (Even though he was okay with me spending all day in the hot sun picking cotton!) Maybe that's one reason I've always paid attention to being ladylike—to getting my hair done just right and my makeup just so—to prove to Daddy that wrestling and being a lady could go hand in hand. Maybe that's also why I've drummed into all the girls I've trained that if they want Moolah training and managing them, they've got to abide by my ground rules, the first and foremost one being that they can never forget to act the part of a real lady.

By the way, I think that Daddy came around near the end of his life. In 1950, he was in the hospital and very sick with lung cancer. The doctors said there was nothing more they could do for him. He had never seen me wrestle and I desperately wanted him to. He still didn't like that I was wrestling, but he wanted to see me do it, because I think he was curious how I'd do.

While he was in the hospital I was to make my hometown debut at the auditorium in Columbia. The doctors gave permission for my dad to come, and my brothers brought him to ringside in a wheelchair. That night I was scheduled to fight Mae Young, of all people, and I beat her up but good. I kept looking over at my daddy, sitting not too far from where we used to sit when I was a wide-eyed ten-year-old wrestling wannabe, and I kept seeing the happiest man. I hadn't seen my daddy smile that way in a long, long time. I don't know, but I think he changed his mind that night and decided it was okay for me to go after my dream in the ring. If he didn't, I'm sorry, but this is all I ever wanted to do. It was what I was *meant* to do.

Daddy passed away soon after that, and I sure was thankful I'd made him happy that night. It always pleased me to make my dad happy. When I was a teenager, I left my grandma's and moved back in with my dad and brothers. I just wanted to come and help my dad. He was always good about cooking and cleaning the house and all. He'd make the boys do their fair share. I loved to cook, and I loved how much Dad liked the biscuits I used to make for him and the boys.

Still, it was hard living with Daddy and the boys. Because I was the only girl and the youngest, they were all too darned protective of me. I spent all this time dreaming about living an adventurous life—first as an aviator, then as a wrestler—and they all would

hardly let me out of their sight. By then we had left Tookiedoo and were living on Two Notch Road in Columbia, close to the center of town. A block and a half from us was a drugstore where I used to like to go in the evening and get me a milk shake or a Coke float. Almost every night I'd go into that drugstore, and when I looked around quickly, I'd see three or four of my brothers standing outside, peeking through the window to see what I was up to.

In that drugstore I met a boy, Walter Carroll. He was nice, and he had a sparkling new Ford that he would leave with me and let me drive to school. He kept saying, "Let's run away and get married." Now, I was all of fourteen. I didn't know what love was, but I thought, Hmm, I wouldn't have to go through all this mess with my spying brothers and my daddy telling me I can't wrestle if I was married. So one night, I just about surprised the hair off Walter's head when he talked about us getting hitched and I just said, "Well, let's go, then."

Back then, you didn't have to go and apply for a license or take blood tests or anything. You could just go to the justice of the peace, say your vows, and that's it. So that's what we did, Walter and I. Ten months later, our baby Mary was born and I said to myself, That's enough for me. My mama had enough kids for the both of us. It's funny, because when Mary grew up, she tried her hand at wrestling some, and she was darned good, too. But it wasn't in her blood, like it was in mine. Instead, she wanted to have babies and stay at home with them. Now she's had five kids and adopted one other beauti-

ful child. I guess the child-rearing bug skipped a generation between my mama and my daughter.

Of course, my marriage to Walter didn't last but a few more months after Mary came along. Babies ain't ready to go around playing house and having babies. I wouldn't let Walter or having Mary stand in my way, either. I was going on the road to get paid to wrestle and I was gonna be the champ. My daddy still didn't want me to go, just like he wasn't too thrilled when he learned Walter and I had eloped. But I couldn't help myself. I was going out to become a wrestler. Nothing could stop me.

4

THE ROAD

AS A LITTLE GIRL, when I wasn't daydreaming about spending my life in the sky flying planes or in the ring kicking butt, I dreamed of going to Montana. See, I always loved cowboys and cowgirls, and I thought, *If I can ever get to Montana, I'll be riding them horses and singin' cowboy songs.*

Now, what's that old saying? *Be careful what you wish for, you just might get it.* When I first turned pro and made it to Montana, I wasn't too much in love with the place, because the experience of getting there turned me against the state.

In those days, to get to your matches, you had to hitch a ride with whoever you could. Montana was the destination of my first long trip, and there I was sitting alongside The French Angel in the backseat of a beat-up Ford while a Canadian wrestler sat behind the wheel, guzzling beers and zigzagging across the highway at 110 miles per hour.

I was still a teenager and don't mind admitting that I was scared frozen, praying to God and thinking, *I must love wrestling to go through this.* Next to me, The French Angel was sitting with a little metal tub—we'd call it a foot tub—and it was filled with beer and ice. Now, The French Angel's real name was Maurice Tillet, and he suffered from some glandular disorder that disfigured his features. He was so ugly that he was billed as a "monstrosity." So there I was, an innocent teenager chasing a dream, next to this monster chugging brew, while another beer head took my life in his hands behind the wheel.

Wouldn't you know that, going through those Montana mountains, we got stuck in the snow. Looking back on it now, I wonder if this was some sort of initiation these fellas were putting me through, but that never occurred to me then. I was just scared to death.

Once we got stuck, there was nothing for me to do but try and get some shut-eye until we were rescued. As I dozed off, The French Angel and our driver were still drinking beer like it was going out of style.

I don't know how long I was out, but I was awakened by a loud roar. I tell ya, I'll never forget this next sight as long as I live. I opened my eyes and there was a great big bear standing by the car, right next to the window on The French Angel's side. That big bear's head was thrown back while The French Angel leaned out the window and was pouring bottle after bottle of beer down the

bear's mouth. That bear was lapping it up and it roared every time The French Angel finished off a bottle. It was hard to tell who loved the beer more, the bear or the two drunks in the car with me.

"Oh, my God, that bear's going to kill us all!" I cried.

Just then, a snowplow approached; seeing it, the bear made to take off, only he must have been feeling the effects of the alcohol, so he staggered away, looking like he was about to keel over any minute, while the fellas roared in laughter.

That was my welcome to the wacky world of professional wrestling. Now I know that a better introduction couldn't have been had.

In those days, there was no such thing as World Wrestling Entertainment, a big organization that runs everything and treats its performers right. Back then, the country was made up of a lot of different—and even some shady—promoters. They each controlled a territory or region, and together they formed the National Wrestling Alliance so that each could keep control of his own area. If you wanted to wrestle in, say, Boston, you had to do business with a fella named Paul Bowser. My area was controlled by Billy Wolfe, so I had no choice but to hook up with him.

Around this time, I met my dear Daisy Mae. I was playing bass fiddle in a country band with one of my brothers and Daisy Mae was sixteen at the time and dating the guy who played violin for us. From the moment I met her, I could tell she was sweet and

kindhearted, a pretty girl with the widest, most innocent eyes and skinniest legs you've ever seen. "What do you do?" she asked.

I told her I was getting ready to go on the road and wrestle. Her eyes lit up. "That's what I want to do!" she said. We started a life-long friendship. I told her I'd learn to wrestle and then teach her. Meantime, I left my baby, Mary, in her care. Mary loved Daisy Mae instantly; to this day, Daisy Mae is her "Nanny."

Leaving Mary behind was hard, but I was comforted by the fact that she'd be cared for by someone who loved her. Besides, I had no choice. I just had to pursue my dream of wrestling. It was in my blood. I was in for quite a shock at first, because life on the road back then was pretty short on glory.

Now, you know that I'm kind to everyone who is kind to me, but I quickly found out that Billy Wolfe didn't have too many kind bones in his body. To my way of thinking, he was a despicable human being. Even so, I knew I had to deal with him—at least at first—to realize my dream. When I first went to see him, he looked me up and down my five-foot, four-inch frame. "You're just too small to be a lady wrestler," he said. "You should go home and get yourself a job as a secretary so you can sit on some lawyer's knee."

"Listen, I'm gonna be a wrestler," I said. "And I'm gonna be the best damned one you ever seen."

Wolfe saw that I wouldn't be turned away, so he got me a book-ing at the Boston Arena for my first match. It was May 26, 1949, and

the main event featured Juanita Coffman going against Mae Weston. I was going against June Byers on the undercard. A ringside seat that night cost all of $2.40. I'm afraid I didn't give those big spenders sitting ringside much of a show. June gave me a good going over. *That's okay*, I thought, *I'll get even with her later.* Sure enough, I did.

But it was really tough to begin with. Billy never really cared about the girls. You'd get fifty dollars a week, whether you wrestled once or twenty times. And it was usually twenty times. Now out of

that whole fifty dollars, you'd have to pay for a motel room, your food and gas, plus I'd want to send money back home for my baby. Oftentimes I'd drive all night to get to a booking, and looking to save a few dollars, I'd do without stopping to eat or sleep in a motel. When I got too drowsy, I'd pull over on the side of the road to catch a catnap, or I'd pull the car over and sprint around it while screaming like a wild woman just to shock my system awake. And when my stomach grumbled too much from hunger, I'd stop at a diner and swipe me some ketchup to eat just so I wouldn't pass out.

Billy was married to Mildred Burke, my idol while I was growing up. Billy never set out to be a women's wrestling promoter. In fact, when Mildred first asked him to train her to wrestle, Billy asked a male wrestler to body-slam her so hard she would stop bothering him about getting in the ring. Well, the story goes that Mildred turned the tables on that man and actually body-slammed him, making a believer out of Billy. Even so, I never did get to wrestle Mildred because, like I said before, Billy would only let her wrestle girls that he wanted her to face, and I think he knew I might be too tough for her.

Billy was something else. At this time, see, he had a lot of girls in his stable, including Mildred, June Byers, and me, along with Mae Young and another girl named Nell Stewart. But we traveled in two separate groups. So when Billy would go with Mildred's group, he'd sleep with her. But sometimes he'd go with June's group, and

that's when he'd get her or Nell in bed. June and Nell wanted the best bookings, so they slept with Billy whenever he liked.

These were wild times—and there were a lot of wild girls on the road back then. Mae was one of them. She used to like to go out drinking till all hours, smoking cigars and picking fights with big, bruising men in dark honky-tonks. She'd always laugh later about that expression on their face, a mixture of surprise and shame, just before they hit the floor after she'd conked them upside the head.

Mae and I still laugh about the time she was asleep in the backseat of a car on her way to a match somewhere. And the fella wrestler next to her thought he could take advantage of the moment. So he reached over and put his hand down the front of her shirt. Now, Mae never did fill out up top like some of the other girls. So this guy reached in to cop a feel, stirring Mae awake, and what does she do but matter-of-factly reach down her shirt and whip out her falsies and hand them to the guy! "Here, you want to feel my boobies, knock yourself out!" she said to him. He about had a heart attack! We laugh about that all the time, and I told Mae that when I wrote my book, I'd tell the world about how she whipped out her false titties that night. "Go right ahead," she said proudly.

I was never quite as wild as Mae, although I always got a kick out of her outrageous behavior. I was still a nice, good girl, so I always resisted Billy's advances. If you didn't fall into his arms like he wanted, then you didn't get treated very nicely. I didn't give a

damn whether he gave me a good booking or not. I just wanted experience in the ring. I knew I could make it on my own if I could just learn the ropes a little bit. It's not like I could learn from Billy Wolfe, after all; he didn't have a school for the girls or anything. We'd roll into a new town, and just an hour or two before show time, some of the older girls would show a newer girl a couple of moves. That was the extent of the training.

Now, don't get me wrong. I might have disliked Billy Wolfe, but I wasn't regretting a thing. I was loving every day on the road. I'd begin and end each day by saying my prayers, and there were plenty of times in between that called for prayer, too, but even then, I never wanted to be doing anything else. There's nothing like being young and on the road in America, and I felt like I was living for the first time in my life.

That doesn't mean I totally enjoyed every hairy situation I found myself in. There was the time I was in Utah in the dead of winter with a couple of the midget girls, driving a Chevy station wagon. It was snowing like crazy and that car started sliding all over the road. I started praying, "Oh, Lord, don't take us now," but I kept my prayers to myself because I didn't want to scare the little midgets. Soon enough, I lost control of the car as we rounded a mountain bend. That car skidded right for the edge of a cliff; when it stopped, I couldn't see anything out my windshield but Utah air. I slowly opened my door and my worst fear was realized: We were dangling

over the edge of the cliff, just like you see in the movies. Only this was no movie and I was scared. "Don't nobody move!" I yelled, knowing that a sudden weight shift could send us all over the edge.

Ever so slowly I got out first, and then I opened the back door and had the midgets move over, an inch at a time. "Easy, easy now," I kept telling them. If one of us had jumped out, I think that car would have gone right over the edge. I was afraid to breathe, thinking that just about anything could force that car to go. Finally, when I got them out, I said, "Oh, God, thank you so much."

We spent hours huddled up there together, in the freezing snow, me and the midgets, praying for help. And then I heard a snowplow coming. I can't tell you how many times I've been saved by snowplows! I started waving my arms, but it soon became clear that the snow was so high, the driver couldn't see me. And he damned well couldn't see the midgets. "You wait here," I told them. "Don't touch the car."

I ran across the road, waving my jacket in the air, until the fella inside the plow saw me. I showed him what had happened to us and he couldn't believe it. "Boy, you sure are lucky," he said. He towed the car out from behind. We thanked him and went further on into the blizzard. We had a booking to get to, so I had to go extra fast, even though my knees were still shaking from our near miss. I don't mind telling you, I was playing brave for the sake of those midgets, because I knew I had to lead them, they couldn't lead me.

Another time I was driving a station wagon with two other girls and two midgets to wrestle somewhere out on the Texas prairie. The wagon broke down about fifty miles from where we were going to be wrestling. I found someone who worked on cars in this little town that reminded me of Tookiedoo, and he told me it would take a while to repair the car. Just then, along came a pickup truck loaded with peanuts. I flagged the driver down and told him I'd be glad to pay him for a lift fifty miles down the road.

He was a big, fat, greasy guy. He looked at me, the two other girls, and the two midgets and raised an eyebrow. "What are you all gonna be doing in that town?" he asked.

"We're wrestling there tonight, and we'd be happy to pay you," I said.

He broke into a big, gap-toothed smile. "If you all are wrestlin', you don't have to pay me," he said. "Just let me come and see the wrestlin' show, and I'll be glad to take you."

It was a deal. We hauled our four suitcases out of the truck and then had to go about figuring where we'd sit. After all, there were four girls and four suitcases in a pickup piled high with peanuts. "Hmm," said the trucker. "How we gonna do this?"

"I don't know, but as long as my midgets are okay, the rest of us can sit anywhere," I said.

Well, we put one of the girls with the midgets in the cab with the fat guy, and me and the other girl got in the back, with the suit-

cases. You've never seen so many peanuts! By the time we made the fifty-mile trip, I wasn't hungry, either, because I nibbled on peanuts the whole way there. We got to the arena as the bell was ringing. I was so proud that we got there to do our show, I walked in holding the fat truck driver's arm and I told the usher that this was a VIP; they put him ringside, and after the show, he drove us all the way back, where the station wagon was repaired and ready to go. Then it was on to the next show.

In early 1950, after a few months on the road, I was back in Columbia. When I wasn't spending time with Mary—she was just the cutest little thing—I was by my daddy's bedside at the hospital. Billy called from Columbus, Ohio, saying he needed me there pronto for a match. Like a good little soldier, I got in the car and drove through the night to Ohio. I spent all my money on the road, but I got there in time for the match, which I won, despite dislocating my shoulder. Afterward, there was an urgent call for me from my sister-in-law. Daddy had died.

Heartbroken, I went to Billy's hotel room. "Billy, my dad passed away," I said. "Could you loan me a hundred dollars so I can make his funeral?"

His exact words were: "You just left home two days ago. What do you want to do, go home and hold his hand?"

I knew he was no good, but this was even below him. I stared at him, dumbfounded.

"No," he said. "I don't have a hundred dollars to lend you."

Through clenched teeth, I managed to blurt out: "I hope you die in the damned gutter and the worms eat your body before they find you!" And I stormed out of there, sobbing.

In the hotel lobby, the wrestler Jack LaRue and his wife, Cecelia Evans, saw me crying. When I told them what was wrong, bless their hearts, Cecelia opened her purse. "Here's a hundred-dollar bill," she said. "If you ever get it, send it back. If you don't, you can have it."

I hugged them both. "Thank you very much," I said, "but you will get your money back."

I got to the airport and flew to Washington, D.C., where I met up with one of my brothers and we drove to Columbia for Daddy's funeral. And I never went back to Billy Wolfe, though I did make sure to repay Jack and Cecelia.

Back then, I don't mind telling you that Billy Wolfe headed my enemies' list. All he cared about was money. He worked us like slaves. But it's a funny thing what the years can do to grudges. As time passed, my heart went out to him from afar. He and Mildred broke up, and then June Byers, just to spite him, married Billy's son. I'm so glad I never got tangled up in that mess.

After I left him, and after Mildred bolted, Billy was trying to come up with the new tough girl—the next champ. It must have driven him crazy when I went on to win the championship. Anyway, he adopted this girl named Janet Wolfe, who was supposed to be real tough. Well, she was in a tag-team match against Mae Young and Ella Waldeck; during the match, she landed wrong, hit her head, and died. She hemorrhaged to death. I know Mae still feels the pain of that night, and keeps asking herself, *I wonder if I'm the one who did that?* But it was an even greater tragedy for Billy Wolfe. He took up with a very young girl, who died while he was with her. He was a broken man.

But I didn't know how it would turn out for Billy when I left him. I just left because nothing was worth being treated like a piece of meat. "You'll get nowhere without me!" Billy warned when I stormed out on him that night. I remember thinking, *We'll just see about that, won't we?*

Lillian Ellison

5
MOOLAH
IS BORN

YOU KNOW HOW YOU START TELLING STORIES from your past and sometimes you get all gloomy for what you used to have? Or for those possibilities that stretched out before you when you were young? Well, that's one reason I never did go in much for telling old stories. By now you might get the picture: I'm the type of gal who looks forward, who doesn't dwell on what I've got no control over.

That's one of the reasons Mae and I—and even my damn midget Katie, the baby among us at fifty-seven years old—get all frustrated when we're around people our own age. They sit around and tell stories and get all sad for what they convince themselves were the good old days. Well, go on out and create some good *new* days! I said to Mae when we were talking about this here book, "I'm going to tell stories all right—but there ain't gonna be no sense of regret to them. I lived this life, and I'd live it again."

Lillian Ellison

That's not to say there weren't hardships, and I'll be honest about them and with you, too. Like when it comes to men. I'm not going to dwell on my marriages here, sugar, but I'm not going to flinch from telling you what you need to know. And what you need to know is that toward the end of my time with Billy Wolfe, I met Johnny Long, who would become my second husband.

Johnny was a big wrestling star around the Carolinas and Baltimore back in the late 1940s and early 1950s. Oh, he was a real looker. I used to call him my Joe Palooka, because he was built: fifty-four-inch shoulders above a thirty-two-inch waist. When I first met Johnny, he was kind enough to teach me some wrestling moves. Remember, this was back when Billy was working us girls like slaves and not teaching us a damn thing.

So along came this gorgeous hunk, and for the first time I was learning how to protect myself in the ring. Johnny taught me how to take a bump, how to land just so in order to jump right back up and hardly feel a thing. Today, I really give Johnny a lot of the credit for the champion wrestler I turned out to be.

He was a great wrestling teacher, but that didn't mean our marriage was going to work. We got along fine at first, but then we had some conflict. Eventually, Johnny wanted me to stay home and be a housewife. Now, I have nothing but support for women who choose to raise kids and work at home—and don't kid yourself, staying home and raising kids is work. Heck, that's the choice my daughter,

Mary, wound up making. She tried her hand at wrestling and was damned good at it, too, but she decided that what she really wanted to do was have babies. And like I said before, she ended up giving me the greatest gift imaginable—my darling grandbabies, who have grown up and gone on to produce my great-grandkids.

Just as Mary couldn't imagine not having kids, I couldn't imagine not wrestling back then. I always told Johnny, "I'm gonna pursue my profession." In fact, I used to say that a lot, and I'd get a kick over just how uncomfortable it would make men. After all, this was a time when men expected women to be wifely, barefoot and pregnant in the kitchen. Of course part of their discomfort might have been due to what I'd say next, if they didn't already know what line of work I was in: "I'm in the world's *oldest* profession, darlin'," I'd say, batting my eyelids. "I'm just a professional girl." Almost without fail, big, tough, strong fellas would just about have heart attacks right in front of me when they heard that.

Anyway, one day long before we got married, Johnny was showing me some moves in the ring when I was struck by an idea. Since Billy wasn't teaching any of us a damned thing, why didn't Johnny and I train some of the girls? Well, Billy got a big laugh out of this, especially when he heard that we'd charge a few cents for the service. "You'll never do nothing," he said.

Once I had had enough and stormed out on Billy, Johnny said he knew a promoter who would be happy not only to take me on

but also the girls we were training. We had Daisy Mae, of course, and Ella Waldeck (who we gave the ring name Jackie Lee) and Katherine Simpson (who called herself Katherine the Great). Johnny called Jack Pfeffer, who didn't have any female wrestlers to promote. So he was thrilled when he heard from Johnny.

Jack Pfeffer was one of the all-time great characters in the crazy world of wrestling, and that's saying something. He was a little Russian Jew who spoke with a thick accent. He snuck into the United States during the Holocaust—it sends a shiver up my spine just to think about it. He hid in the boiler room of a ship that came over from Europe, and that's how he escaped the tragic fate that many of his family met. He always wore the same heavy overcoat, no matter the weather, and he always had the worst body odor you could imagine. He had long gray hair that, in the right light, looked platinum blond; from a distance, he looked like Marilyn Monroe if she'd lost an acid fight.

Jack was a good guy, though. If he promised you something, that was what you got. But you never got more. At one point I was making one hundred dollars a week wrestling for Jack, and he'd make the other wrestlers who got rides with me chip in for gas. Of course he'd make all sorts of promises about how you were going to get a percentage of the gate if it exceeded such and such number, but it never did seem to happen. Still, he guaranteed the one hundred dollars a week and that's what I got. At that time in this busi-

ness, it was rare to find a promoter who kept his commitments. Jack certainly was a contrast to Billy Wolfe, who would send you into a town—another promoter's territory—and tell you to sleep with that promoter to get your money. Billy knew better than to propose that to me, because he knew I'd just as soon wrestle for free.

Jack stood out in other ways, too. He was ahead of his time. You know, every week now I tune in to Vince's wrestling shows, and I swear I can't help but see Jack's legacy. Vince has done more for wrestling than anybody, in terms of turning it into showbiz, but Jack Pfeffer was really the first one to see that wrestling was really entertainment. He decided to give the people what they wanted,

and he knew they wanted a story, they wanted colorful characters in wild getups, characters they could love or hate.

So Jack would stay up all night sewing capes with sequins and rhinestones and all kinds of flashy stuff for his wrestlers to wear. He's the guy who discovered the legendary Buddy Rogers, and gave him the catchy nickname Nature Boy.

Buddy Rogers was an out-and-out star. He had a knack for what we call ring showmanship. Remember how, when I was all of ten years old, I felt that Mildred Burke had a way of getting a whole auditorium to focus their attention on her every move? That's ring showmanship, and no one was better at it than Buddy Rogers. It's no coincidence that around this time a little boy in Louisville, Kentucky, was growing up, soaking up Buddy Rogers's presence and witnessing how he carried himself and captivated giant crowds. That boy's name was Cassius Clay, who went on to become known as Muhammad Ali.

Ring showmanship can be learned, but it can't be taught. I learned it from watching Mildred Burke and Buddy Rogers, seeing how they owned every moment in the ring. You'd watch them and forget they had an opponent. It's an attitude. Stone Cold Steve Austin has it. You have to learn to let yourself go and not to worry about being liked. People love Stone Cold because he's comfortable being who he is. I don't want to say he's a redneck; he's more what I'd call country tough.

Of all people, Vince McMahon Jr. has this sense of ring showmanship. Vince was always a sweet, lovely boy, but who knew he'd be able to command so much respect and attention inside the ring? It's because he soaked up examples while he was growing up. I'll let you in on a little secret. You've seen Vince come strutting into the ring? That's the Buddy Rogers strut. The first time I saw him do it, I thought Buddy's ghost had taken over that boy's body.

"Vince!" I said. "I thought Buddy Rogers was dead!"

He smiled. "I didn't think anybody would notice that," he said.

When I first hooked up with Jack Pfeffer, though, I didn't know much about ring showmanship. In fact, I didn't even look like much of a wrestler. I was five feet four and maybe 118 pounds. Most of the other girls were much bigger. Jack looked me up and down and said in that thick Yiddish accent, "You too tiny to be a vestler."

"Well, I am one," I said. Around about then, I took to bulking myself up. I started eating steak and mashed potatoes with butter every chance I got. Every morning and night, I drank a glass of pure cream with two tablespoons of Hershey's syrup and three raw eggs in it. How'd it taste? Darn good, sugar, because I knew it was turning me into a championship wrestler.

Not that I got much of a chance to wrestle at first. Jack had come up with one of his famous brainstorms. First, he said the name Lillian Ellison wouldn't do. Not flashy enough. He started asking me questions, like "Vy do you vant to vestle all the time?"

Finally, annoyed, I blurted out, "For the money! I want to wrestle for the moolah!"

Jack broke into a big, gap-toothed smile, bad breath and all. "That's vhat ve'll name you—Moolah!" he said. Only there was one more thing: "Lillian," he said, "I vant to make you a slave girl. Slave Girl Moolah." He sat back, satisfied with himself.

"I don't care what you make me, just make me some money," I said, and he laughed again. He went on to tell me that while I was bulking myself up, I'd be Slave Girl Moolah, the valet for Buddy Rogers. Gorgeous George had already made having a girl valet part of his act, and the fans seemed to love it. She'd come out and spray the ring with perfume and give George a little massage, all to fire up the crowd. Now I'd be doing the same with Buddy Rogers, the greatest wrestler

SLAVE GIRL MOOLAH WORLD'S JR. HEAVYWEIGHT CHAMPION

in the world, and Jack was giving me the chance to be Buddy's partner and learn from watching the best night in and night out.

So I began the 1950s traveling with Buddy. Johnny Long and I
were history, because I just couldn't resist the call of the road. Besides, I realized Johnny was a womanizer when I caught him making out with one of my girls on the stage of the arena in Hillsboro,
North Carolina. I drove her home from the show, and we stopped
in a heavily wooded area off the highway, and let's just say we had
us a nice little talk. I told her to pack her bags when we got back to
Columbia and to hop the first Greyhound out of town, if she knew
what was good for her. The next time I saw her, she was with none
other than Billy Wolfe. It made sense to me instantly because she

would fit in perfectly with Billy—she's got that type of class. Not much, in other words. So I was out there on the road again, feeling free. At this time in America, the hemlines on dresses went to the floor and ladies wore hats and gloves when they went out in public. There I was, in the ring, wearing a leopard-print costume that left little to the imagination so that the fans who flocked to see Buddy would see me, primping and waiting on him, standing by my man. Outside the ring, well, that's where the problems started.

See, Buddy was kind of wild, and that just wasn't my style. He wanted us to be just too close, if you know what I'm saying, which was against Jack Pfeffer's rules. Unlike Billy Wolfe, Jack didn't want nobody messing with his girls. "No, Buddy, I'm not that way," I'd always tell him when he started to put his sloppy moves on me. "This is my business and I'm here to work, and I don't fool around with somebody in the business."

One day we were in the car on the way to St. Louis. We were maybe fifty miles from the city when Buddy said to me, "I'm goin' to get a motel here, and you're gonna put out or get out."

He thought he had me at his mercy, out there on the Missouri plain. I said, "Stop the damn car."

He slammed on the brakes. I reached in the back for my bag and got out. "You're getting out, right?" he said, like a challenge.

"That's right, and to hell with you," I said.

So I walked down the street until I found a bar. Inside, they directed me toward the bus station. As luck would have it, a bus was just getting ready to leave for St. Louis when I got there. I bought me a ticket, and as I was getting on the bus, here comes Buddy, speeding on up. I just stopped and gave him the Stone Cold Salute—one long finger in the air, and you know which one—and boarded that bus.

Buddy beat me to the auditorium. I got there right when the bell rang to signal the main event—me and Buddy. Jack was chewing his cigar, ticked off. "Vere have you been?" he screamed.

"I'll tell you the whole story later, but you want me to work tonight or not?" I said, brushing past him to change into my costume. Once I got into the ring, I saw a frightened Buddy Rogers. "Please don't tell Jack about what happened," he said. "I'll never do it again."

"I know you won't," I said. "Because I've been telling you for months that I'm not that way."

After I gave my usual 110 percent in the ring, Jack was waiting for me in the dressing room, chomping nervously on his cigar. This was risky, mind you. Buddy Rogers was a big star. If it came down to him or me, I knew I'd be gone. But I didn't care. I believed in myself so much that if I got fired by Jack Pfeffer, I knew I'd get another job.

"I'm not working with Buddy Rogers anymore," I told Jack. I went on to fill him in about what Buddy had been up to. Jack didn't have a lot of color to begin with, but what little he did have I saw

drain from his face in anger. When Buddy came into the dressing room, you could hear Jack cussin' at him throughout the arena. Buddy wouldn't have a valet for a long time.

Meantime, Jack asked me if I'd consider being the slave girl for the Elephant Boy. "Don't you get along good with him?" he asked.

"Yes, he's always been the perfect gentleman with me." The Elephant Boy was Tony Olivas, a giant with big kinky hair. Jack promoted him as "the wrestler from darkest Africa" even though he was Mexican. The Elephant Boy was a sweetheart. My, did we have some fun on the road. Much of it was at poor old Jack Pfeffer's expense.

Like I said, Jack had what we'll call a personal hygiene problem. He kept a tiny room—he called it an apartment—in New York, and I remember once going into the bathroom there. I looked in the tub and you could have just written anything or drawn any pictures in there that you wanted to, it was so full of dust.

Once, we were going from Washington, D.C., to Boston in the Elephant Boy's Ford convertible and Jack was sitting in the front passenger seat. Normally, we'd have the top down to get rid of some of Jack's stench, but it was the dead of winter. We had the heat cranked, but I was in the backseat and all the heat was doing was pushing Jack's stench right back at me. I'd taken some beatings in the ring, but nothing ever came as close to knocking me out as this particular smell.

"Open your window, Jack," I begged.

"It's vinter!" he yelled. "I'm not opening the vindow!"

Well, I thought I'd be smart. When we stopped for gas, I bought some mothballs. On the front console of the car was a little floorboard heater that had two doors on it. While Jack slept we put the bag of mothballs in there, figuring that when we turned on the heat, the mothball smell would kill the Jack Pfeffer smell.

Well, it was a close match between those two aromas, but the mothballs won out. It got so strong, it woke Jack up and he discovered the bag in the heater and cursed us out while we gasped for breath and giggled at the same time. Later, I wasn't laughing when a doctor friend of mine told me that we could have been killed inhaling that stuff, but that just goes to show the lengths we'd go to save ourselves from what Jack gave off.

Bless his soul, Jack was a funny man, and he didn't even know it. Like this one time when we were on our way to Montana; I was driving a Chevy and Buddy Lee—you'll hear a lot about Buddy Lee up ahead—and Jack were following me in a Caddy. The Caddy's front right tire blew out and the next thing I know, Jack is yelling at Buddy. "Vy do you not buy a Chevy like Moolah, then you vouldn't have flat tires!"

As time went on, we all became more and more popular, and that was thanks to Jack's vision. He took to calling his traveling company "a band of freaks," and that was never a truer selling point than when I discovered The Lady Angel for Jack.

One night after a match in Jacksonville, a big girl by the name of Tommi Huckaby came to the dressing room and introduced herself. She wanted to be a wrestler. Now, Tommi was a sight. A few years before, when she was sixteen, someone she knew had a private plane and flew her from Florida to Macon, Georgia. Well, when she got off the plane she walked straight into the propeller and it slashed up her face like you wouldn't believe—took her nose clean off and skinned her scalp in one ferocious motion.

Oh, it was horrible. She had all sorts of plastic surgery done, but there was no way to fix it back right. She had scars all over her face, and what little bit of hair she had just came back in patches. I decided to take her back to Columbia and train her, turn her into a wrestler. She wasn't an easy one to train, either. She was a big girl—five-eleven—with a huge bust and almost as bald-headed as Stone Cold. She wasn't fat, just big, and kind of stiff—not a natural athlete. We spent hours and hours in the gym until I felt confident enough to tell Jack about her.

"Next show, I'm gonna bring my new protégée," I told him.

"Vhat? Who do you mean?" he asked.

"I'm bringing The Lady Angel. Guess what, Jack? She's bald-headed!"

He just about screamed. "Bring her here now!" he cried. If I knew him, he was already plotting just how to promote her.

The next show was in Toledo, Ohio, and once Jack took one look

at The Lady Angel, he was off and running. He plastered the town with flyers advertising her as "The Ugliest Woman in the World," and from then on, she wore that championship belt proudly. We used to have a lot of fun on the road, too. When she wasn't wrestling, The Lady Angel wore a dark floppy wig. We used to like to put it on Jack—especially when he started dozing off. Back then, it was rare for a woman to be wearing a wig and almost unheard of for her to be bald underneath one. So we'd pull up to a tollbooth, and just as The Lady Angel was paying the toll, I'd reach over and yank off her wig. You should've seen how wide the eyes of the toll taker would become as we sped off, laughing like a pack of hyenas!

Back then, we'd laugh like that to let off steam on the road because we were always finding ourselves in some sticky situations. Once in Oklahoma City I was the Elephant Boy's slave girl and there was a lot of racial stuff going on at that time. The audience didn't know the Elephant Boy was Mexican; he was so dark-skinned, I guess they thought he was black. So I'd come into the ring with him and comb his hair and tease it up, get it all bushy, and I'd kiss him on the cheek. Well, that didn't go over too well, this petite white woman in a skimpy Jane of the Jungle costume kissing in public someone they all thought was a black man.

When I came out of the ring, there was quite a crowd jostling around me, and then suddenly there was this giant man standing in front of me. I remember him as about twelve feet tall, but that

can't be right. That must just be how I felt at the time, all small and vulnerable to him. I saw something glitter in his hand as it came toward me, and the next thing I knew I heard the tearing of my dress—that's when it dawned on me that he had a knife and was trying to stab me! Well, if it hadn't been for the bra that I had on, he would have cut me good. As it was, he cut through the straps of my bra and I had nicks all the way down my side. Luckily, the people standing around saw what he was doing and grabbed him and the cops took him away, but that was a close one. As they carried him off I stood there, half-naked, and said, "Well, he saw what he wanted to see."

As rowdy as World Wrestling Entertainment shows get nowadays, the fans are a lot calmer now that they know it's entertainment. If Stone Cold or Triple H had been wrestling back then, they would have had to have a security team surrounding them at all times. I mean, the short walk from the dressing room to the ring was always dangerous—you were always a split second away from having a knife stuck in you or from getting shot at. That's what happened to my friend Mae Weston. She wrestled down in Florida, and she played the Bass Brothers' mother. They were big villains at the time. She got shot at one night in Mobile, Alabama, just walking from the dressing room to the ring with her supposed two sons. The bullet grazed her head and just missed killing her. Now think about the way people hate Stephanie McMahon—who is really one of the sweetest, dearest girls on the planet. But, like her dad and her brother, she knows how to sell her character in the ring. If she was wrestling forty or fifty years ago, with the way she can raise fans' passions, she'd have been flirting with disaster every night.

Once, in Montana, a burly guy sitting ringside got the damn fool idea to come at me. After I took care of him, he tried to sue me; the case was thrown out because he was the instigator, but I've kept the court papers all these years just for a good chuckle now and again: "Plaintiff was greatly injured about the face, neck and head and . . . has been unable to wear or use his denture or dental plate. . . ."

By 1951, I was no longer playing slave girl to anyone. People were showing up to see me wrestle. They were pelting me with rotten eggs and beer cans, cussing me. And guess what? I loved it. I still get goose bumps when I think about the walk from the dressing room to the ring, how I'd come down that tunnel underneath the stairs and hear the muffled screams and music and then come out on the runway leading to the squared circle to have a loud chorus of boos just raining down on me.

Everyone has always asked me, how could you like being booed? Well, I didn't care if they booed or if they cheered. Either way, I knew I was doing my job right. As long as they were making noise for me, that meant I was reaching them, that meant they couldn't take their eyes off me, just like I couldn't take my eyes off Mildred Burke all those years ago, just like so many fans could never take their eyes

off Buddy Rogers. It meant I *had* them. And the funny thing was, the same fans who were cussing and booing me would be the ones hugging and patting me on the back when I came out of the ring, the ones saying, "You did a great job tonight, Moolah."

I guess I had a way of getting crowds riled up. A couple of times I even started mini-riots. Once, in Texas, The Lady Angel busted my head open and I just lost all control when I saw my own blood. I tossed her outside the ring and started to put an honest-to-God whuppin' on her in the middle of the audience, so the cops came running. Well, they couldn't contain me. I knocked the cap off one, and I flipped another roly-poly guy over a row of chairs. Someone took a photo of me being led away by the cops. A few days later, it was the cover of *Rasslin'* magazine under the headline: THE WORLD'S MOST HATED WOMAN: BELIEVE IT OR NOT—THIS IS SLAVE GIRL MOOLAH IN THE IRON GRIP OF THE COPS AFTER HER BLOODY MATCH WITH THE LADY ANGEL. A bloody match it was. All hell broke loose, and I ended up having to cool off in a jail cell for a few hours. When Jack came to get me out, I explained the situation to him. "The cops shouldn't have entered into it," I said, still steaming. "I'm supposed to do what I'm supposed to do. She busted my head open, so it was time for me to do hers." Jack just wanted me to keep my mouth shut long enough to get in the car and get on our way to the next gig.

It was always a special time when the next gig was in Memphis. We'd get into town and without fail my phone would ring and it would be Jerry Lee Lewis, wanting to come down and see the show. Jerry Lee came backstage and introduced himself the first time he saw me wrestle, and we struck up quite a friendship after that. I'd let him know when I was putting on a show in Memphis, and he'd come by, just like he'd tell me when he'd be playing near Columbia. Like I mentioned before, I'm a country musician myself, and

Jerry and I got to where he'd come by the house in Columbia, and we'd have a jam session to end all jam sessions, Jerry on the piano, me on the bass fiddle or guitar.

He was a crazy character, that's for sure. You'd be sitting next to him in a crowded restaurant not thinking anything when he'd hear a song come on the radio—even if it was only from a passing car—and the next thing you know, he's hopping up onto the table and dancing like a fool, just like he'd do on top of his piano—only in a restaurant he'd be stomping on everybody's food. But that was Jerry; when the mood hit, he had to go with it. You know, he came from a very religious background (his first cousin is the preacher Jimmy Swaggart), and watching him, I always thought that the way music took over his whole being was just like what happened to those people in church who'd be struck by God and start speaking in tongues.

Another young musician used to like to come to our Memphis shows, but he was nothing like the outgoing, hyper Jerry Lee. In fact, nobody had yet heard of Elvis Presley when he showed up, dressed in nicely pressed slacks and a button-down shirt. He was driving a truck at the time and singing in some area honky-tonks, trying to make it. But he was just the most quiet, polite boy you'd ever want to meet. I used to tease him and call him my Sunday-school boy. Everything was "yes, ma'am" and "no, ma'am." And he really loved his wrestling. "Moolah, think I could become a wrestler?" he'd ask me.

"Darlin'," I'd say, "I don't know about that, but I know you're meant to entertain people. I have a feeling it's gonna be with that voice of yours."

He'd smile and say, "I guess you're right, but I sure do wish I could wrestle, too." Once I told him he should go and become a big singing star—who knew how big he'd become!—and then he could come to me and we'd arrange for his debut inside the squared circle. He seemed to like that idea.

As Elvis got to be a bigger and bigger star, we were in touch less and less. I'd get Christmas cards from Colonel Parker, and here and there a phone call. As the years went on it broke my heart what happened to that sweet boy. Fame and fortune can be a terrible thing if you don't keep your wits about you, and Elvis became a prisoner of his fame and a victim to drinking and drugging. I think back to those nights in that dressing room in Memphis; I can see Elvis's smooth face plain as day, with his wide eyes, soaking up the stories I told about life on the wrestling circuit. I wish now I knew then about his fate and could have warned him to take care of himself, 'cause nobody else did.

A third singer gave me a whirlwind of a romance for about four months in 1952. Hank Williams Sr. was singing in Oklahoma, and I took in the show. Turns out he was a big wrestling fan and recognized me in the club that night. He introduced himself, and we spent the whole night talking. When I realized how late it was get-

ting, he said, "I got nowhere to be," explaining that he'd just separated from his wife, Audrey.

So Hank and I started dating. He was a real sweet guy who treated me good. Only problem was, he drank all the time. One shot and he'd become a different person, all wild and uptight. Then I started to find out he was into the hard stuff, too—heroin. I told him, "I can't tolerate that," but Hank had a sickness called addiction. I don't mean this to be insulting, but when I think of what happened to Elvis and Hank, I know I'm right when I say that men can't take the punishment that women can. Oh, they can put on a good front, but I really believe that men have always depended on quick fixes—whether it's drinking, drugging, or skirt chasing—to help them cope. I really do believe that women roll with the punches better. Think a man can withstand the torture of childbirth? Gimme a break. He'd be calling for drugs to knock him out at the first hint of a labor pain.

Hank was not tough, and he was living a hard life. People don't realize just how hard it was in those days to be a country singer. He was traveling from town to town in the backseat of his Caddy; it was a life of no rest. He started doing the heroin just so he could sleep.

Still, he was a sweet guy, and I really did love him. One time he was playing in Oklahoma City, and after the show he sat down next to me in his dressing room.

"I want to ask you something," he said.

"What?"

"Will you marry me?"

I was stunned silent. I thought to myself, *Hank Williams just asked me to marry him.* I couldn't say nothing, but a million thoughts were rumbling around my brain. At the time I was making a hundred dollars a week with Jack and I thought for a minute, *Now maybe I can get further ahead.* That's how girls in those days improved their station in life—by hitching on with a man. I was also thinking that poor Hank had just gotten done with Audrey and he just wanted to marry somebody—anybody. That he wanted an answer right away led me to think this wasn't about wanting to marry *me* so much as needing to hear a *yes* from somebody.

"Well, let's slow down," I said, and I remember his shoulders sagging. "Let's just think about this."

We didn't talk much more about it that night, and I headed back to Columbia the next day. I was still thinking about accepting Hank's proposal the next time I came off the road, when I went on the road with him. That's when I saw firsthand just how much he was drinking and drugging. Mind you, his heroin use wasn't because he was some crazy partyer; he used it as medicine, but the grip it had on him was a sickness nonetheless.

He was still trying to get me to marry him, but we came up on a deal breaker. Hank started insisting that I give up wrestling and travel

with him. "If you want to stay in the wrestling business, I'll buy you a damned town and you can promote your own shows," he said.

"That's not what I want," I said. "I want to wrestle."

"Darling," he kept trying, "I'll build you a mansion on the side of a hill. Anything you want."

"I don't know how many ways to say this," I repeated. "I want to wrestle."

"Well, if you're Mrs. Hank Williams, you are not going to wrestle," he said. Now, you know by now how I react when some man starts to telling me what I'm going to do. Normally, I drop the old Stone Cold on him. I guess I really did love Hank, though, because I was still considering it.

"Hank, did I tell you that you couldn't play music anymore if we got married?" I asked him.

"No," he said.

"Well, that's how I feel about wrestling, darlin'."

We looked at each other through sad eyes. We knew it was over. I went back to Columbia. Now, of course, I'm glad it didn't work out, because it would have just been more sorrow and headaches for me. But I knew then I was giving up a really good man, and I was sad. About two months later, I heard the news. Hank had been found dead in his car. Overdose. I'm not a drinker by any stretch of the imagination, but I tossed back a shot or two in honor of him.

Like Elvis, Hank was a sweet man through and through, but neither could handle the cards that life dealt them. Both of them just got so weak in mind, body, and soul, they got to a point where nothing mattered anymore except the escape they found in that crap they put into their bodies. Even as I mourned them I vowed to be strong in my own mind and to never mess with this life that God had given me.

After Hank's death, I threw myself into my work. I barnstormed the country with Jack Pfeffer and his merry band of freaks, although there had been some changes in the cast of characters. Long gone was Buddy Rogers, after he and Jack had had a falling out. In was Buddy Lee, a strapping, blond-headed wrestler Jack was grooming to replace Buddy Rogers. In fact, Buddy Lee was really an Italian from the Bronx by the name of Pino. But Jack saw a similarity between him and Buddy Rogers, even though Buddy Lee was not nearly as good a wrestler, so he named him "Nature Boy" Buddy Lee and made him one of the focal points of the show.

I didn't know it at the time, but this New York Italian would go on to become the love of my life. He'd be with me when I became champ within the next few years, and he'd be there for about a decade thereafter. We'd go on to have us some times—some good, some bad, but it was never, ever boring. Most of all, what I didn't know when Jack first introduced me to Buddy Lee was that this bulky blond boy would be the reason my relationship with Jack Pfeffer would end. I was about to do some growing up but quick.

6

THE CHAMPION

I DON'T MIND TAKING ADVICE, but did you ever stop and think about just how often people *tell* you to do something, almost like a demand? I never did understand that. My damn midget Katie and Mae are two of my best friends, and I'm always offering them my advice, but I don't ever put a condition on it—I don't ever say, "You've got to do such and such or else." That's not how relationships should work. Instead, I've always tried to tell them what I think. If Mae's being a damned fool, I'll be the first to tell her, but then I'm going to support her in whatever foolish caper she decides to go ahead with.

Well, I don't think that most people deal with one another that way. Whether it was Daddy and my brothers telling me I couldn't wrestle or get married, or whether it was Johnny Long or Hank telling me I had to stay home and be a good little wifey, seems like

Lillian Ellison

I've always had to fight back against the demands others were placing on me. Don't get me wrong; whenever other people insisted I do a certain thing, I knew it was usually because they really and truly had my best interests at heart. They were trying to protect me, I guess. But I also knew what I felt inside, and to ignore that would be to disobey myself. By the way, I don't think any of this is too uncommon. I'm sure others have gone through it. Sometimes, people love us so much they try to turn us into what they want us to be, instead of sitting back and letting us figure out things for ourselves.

I guess that's what led to me leaving sweet old Jack Pfeffer. I have no doubt that Jack, unlike Billy Wolfe, cared for me, just as he cared for all his wrestlers. And, in general, I sure do appreciate now just how much he tried to protect his girls. But back then, Jack grew to be too protective, and I rebelled against that, because I wasn't put on this earth to need some man to shield me from anything, no matter how kindly he was. No way, no how.

What happened is that Buddy Lee and I started flirting, on the road. And Jack started seething. He wouldn't let the two of us so much as talk. If we were all in the same car, he'd sit between us and his smell would make it impossible for us to turn our heads to look past him and so much as look at each other. When we were all part of the same traveling show, Jack would stake out the lobby all night long, making sure one of us wasn't sneaking over to the other's room. If Buddy was in a different town, Jack would pay the hotel manager to write down all the calls that came in. First thing the next morning, I'd get accused.

"Buddy kept calling you last night, and you kept calling him," Jack would say.

"So what?" I'd say. "Can't we talk? We're just talking."

He never let up. Sometimes, he'd have the hotel manager listen in on our calls. It's funny—I really don't think I would have fallen for Buddy if it weren't for how hysterical Jack was about all this. The one thing that bonded me and Buddy together, in addition to wrestling, was Jack's paranoia. You see it with kids today, how, when their parents forbid them from doing something, you can bet your bottom dollar that it's the one thing they have to do. That's how it was with Jack. Under other circumstances, Buddy and I might have just been friends. But Jack drove us into each other's arms.

Maybe that's why my relationship with Buddy turned out to be so passionate. Like I said, we had good and bad times, but no boring times. Maybe that's because the way we got started was so crazy, so full of sneaking around and fighting with Jack. We didn't know what it was like to have a normal, calm relationship. So we went on throughout the years to have some terrible rows, but there was always an underlying friendship there, because that's also how we started. In fact, even after we divorced in 1970, we stayed close friends until Buddy's death in early 1999.

Anyway, Jack just got out of hand. I know he meant well, but despite my pleading, he just couldn't let me alone. One day Buddy said, "Why are you putting up with this? Why don't you just leave?"

Now, as you know, by this point I'd already done my share of leaving. I'd left home, I'd left my darling baby, I'd left a couple of husbands, not to mention that no-good Billy Wolfe. So I knew I could do it. But I thought, I've been with Jack a long time. I hate to just up and leave.

So I tried one last time to work it out. Jack wasn't what you'd call a guy who you could reason things with. I guess I should have expected his reaction when I said, "Jack, if you're going to be arguing every day about what I do and what I don't, I'd just rather go on home." That was too much like a threat for Jack's liking, I guess. He exploded—almost literally. I mean, his eyes bulged, and he actually jumped up into the air and yelled, "Just go home! You can be replaced!" He went on, screaming about how I'd never wrestle again. Well, you know me. When somebody says I can't do something, that's a personal challenge. So at that instant I was no longer interested in staying with Jack Pfeffer. I was interested in showing him a thing or two.

So I packed the car and met Buddy in New York. We wound up getting married and made our way back down to Columbia to start a new life together.

I was already training girls in Columbia, and Buddy would help me with that. Then, we figured, we'd get us some wrestling shows and be on our way. Only it turned out to be more complicated than that. Jack Pfeffer was a pretty powerful little king in wrestling, and it turned out that none of the other promoters wanted to cross him.

Like I said, this was well before World Wrestling Entertainment came along. There were plenty of promoters all over the country, each one with a region. Well, Buddy and I got on the horn with them and lined up all sorts of bookings. But as those dates approached, without fail, the promoters would call up and cancel on us. Turns out, they had all called Jack Pfeffer, and he was flexing his muscles. And he had some leverage on them, too.

See, at that time wrestling wasn't considered a "show" like it is now. Nowadays, people tune in and they know there's a script, they know we're playing characters for their entertainment. But back then, the audience was convinced it was real. So if you were a rival promoter and you crossed Jack, he'd threaten to blow the whistle on you. He'd print up flyers telling everyone that your show was a fake, even though it really wasn't. We were still throwing one another through the ropes, after all; if you didn't know how to wrestle, if you weren't an athlete, you could get mighty hurt. But all the other stuff—the characters and their byplay—that was added for the entertainment value. And even though he did the same stuff, Jack was telling anyone who would call that he'd publicize all this if they gave me and Buddy work. Other promoters were scared that

information like that, if it got around, would kill their houses, meaning no one would show up and they'd go broke.

So we couldn't get a job. Times were tough. This was one sad time in my life, even though I was happy being with Buddy. But it was just such a struggle. I'd just bought a home in Columbia, the last place I owned before I moved to where I am now, my estate on Moolah Drive, and I had payments coming due and neither of us was working, neither one of us.

Buddy tried to do little things, handyman-type stuff. And he opened a service station that brought in a few dollars here and there. I took to selling cosmetics door-to-door. Can you picture that? Honestly, it's one of the few times in my life I was doing something just to make ends meet, instead of just doing what I love and getting paid for that. I don't know how people do it, how they get up day after day and trudge off to do work that their heart's not in. If you're not passionate about whatever it is that you're doing, darlin', then that's a sign you ought not to be doing it. I've always been one to believe that if you follow your heart and do what you honestly and truly believe you were meant to do, things will work out. The breaks will come, followed by the money.

Yet there I was, unable to do the thing I loved. We were still training some girls, so I stayed sharp in the ring. But there's nothing like being in that squared circle in front of a packed house, with all eyes glued to you and the boos and the cheers meant only for your ears. Things got tougher, and then a friend of Buddy's offered him construction work, only it was back in the Bronx, where he's from.

So believe it or not, this little country girl packed up her little baby and off we went to New York. I felt like a regular Tammy Wynette, standing by her man. And that's what I'm talking about—that's not me. And that's why living in New York was such a disaster for us, because you can't fit a square peg into a round hole.

You know that saying about New York being a nice place to visit? Well, it sure is true. Living there is an altogether different story. We lived in a cramped apartment in the Bronx, right near the subway. When that damned train would go by, the dishes in the cabinet would rattle and the building would rumble like it was registering on the Richter scale. Plus, the apartment was so small, I couldn't escape the worst of Buddy's qualities: He was a chain-smoker. Back home in Columbia, at least we had a yard and a porch where you could breathe. In the Bronx, the stench of cigarette smoke was always filling my nostrils. I guess I'm just a country gal at heart. I love the clean air, grass, trees, and the way the wind whips through your hair when you're riding a horse. I've always loved horses, because they're just like men, only with none of the problems.

I may have been in the world's biggest city, but I never felt more alone. All of Buddy's old friends called him by his given name, Pino; they were all Italians, like him. He would go out at night with them

and shoot craps under the streetlights, like they do there. He'd come home at three or four in the morning. I'd be so angry, I'd try and let him have it, but we never had time for a good free-for-all fight, because just when I picked up a head of steam, just when I was really telling him off and getting on a roll, that damned train would come roaring by and we'd both have to pause, like we were frozen there, because we couldn't hear each other over the noise. That damn train would make you lose your own train of thought.

Finally, one night when he came waltzing in just before dawn, I'd had enough. I'd tried this for three months, and that was about two months and twenty-seven days too long. He walked in and I could hear one of those damned trains approaching from the distance.

"Buddy, you hear that train comin' by," I said, and then we both stood there, just staring at each other, as the sound drowned out everything but our thoughts.

"What'd you say?" he shouted as the noise of the train trailed off.

That's when I told him. "That's the last time I'm going to hear that here."

"What are you saying?"

"I ain't living up here no more, I can't stand it," I said. "If you want to live with me, I will be in Columbia."

He paused. "Ah, you're just running your mouth," he said, heading off to bed.

Well, we'll just see about that, I thought. The next night, he was coming in at a quarter to four in the morning and I was coming down the stairs with my last suitcase. Mary was already in the car. "Where you going?" he asked.

"I told you," I said. "If you want to live with me, your wife will be at 403 South Prospect Street, Columbia."

He started to say something, but I quickly got behind the wheel and fired up the engine. And then I was off. This was before Interstate 95; I had to take U.S. Route 1 through all sorts of towns, and it felt like it took forever. I drove into the next night and was as

exhausted as I've ever been when I approached my house. But as I got close, I saw that something wasn't right. On the porch swing, there sat a figure. As I pulled up I saw it was Buddy Lee.

He had flown home and beaten me there. Oh, if only I could have driven the car up on that porch without tearing up that car, I would have. But this was what was great about Buddy. He was quite the charmer. He took me in his arms and told me he couldn't let me walk out, that we belonged together; it didn't matter where we were, as long as we were together.

I wasn't mad at him anymore. Until, that is, something dawned on me. "Why didn't you tell me this earlier?" I said. "You could have helped me drive!"

"Are you crazy?" Buddy said, flashing a smile. "I didn't want to drive all that way!"

We still needed a plan. This time Buddy agreed to try one of my ideas. Like I said, the regional promoters who made up the National Wrestling Alliance weren't letting us work because they were afraid of Jack Pfeffer. But there were a lot of smaller promoters around and they were called "the opposition." They'd put on shows on the outskirts of some of the big promoters' territories without giving a cut to the bigger promoter. Wondering why I never thought of this before, I called Tony Santos. He promoted shows just outside Boston. Now, I knew this was a risk, because he and Jack Pfeffer were friendly. But that meant that Tony knew I had made lots of money

for Jack over the years. He said, "Sure, come to Boston."

So Buddy and I got us an apartment in Boston and I started training some girls on the cement floor in our building's basement. Jack threatened to do this and that to Tony, but Tony, bless his heart, stood up to Jack's bullying. Like most bullies, Jack was all bark. "Well, if you expose me, you'll be exposing yourself, too," Tony told him. Needless to say, Tony put us in shows and Jack never made a peep.

Then one night I ran into Paul Bowser at a party. He was the big promoter in the Boston area then. He was talking to some other gentlemen in suits, and I just pushed my way through them and walked right up to him and said, "Mr. Bowser, how come you don't like me?"

He was a bit stunned, but he recognized me. "Moolah," he said. "I love you. I think you're great."

"Well, how come I can't work on your cards?" I said. "How come I don't get to wrestle in Boston?"

"Well, maybe it's because you haven't asked me," he said. Let that be a lesson: I approached that man, figuring what the heck, I had nothing to lose. And it turns out he had just been waiting to be approached! I learned from that little exchange that it never hurts to ask; the worst that will happen is you'll hear the word no.

Three weeks later Moolah and three of her girls were headlining in a Paul Bowser show in Boston. One of those girls was Judy

Grable, who I'd trained and who I was having a good rivalry with in the ring back then. Judy was a good kid, but she was more naive than anyone I ever met. Once, she was visiting us in our Boston apartment and there was a little store just across the Commons. "How about going over to the store and getting us some root beer?" Buddy asked her.

"Oh, no," she said. "That's against my religion, to buy beer. I don't drink it."

I tried to explain to her that I'm not an alcoholic, either, but I drink root beer.

Anyway, Paul Bowser gave us the break we needed. Once we started wrestling in Boston, other promoters came out of the woodwork, which led us to move back to Columbia, where we'd continue to teach wrestling. Meantime, the bookings started coming: Atlanta, North Carolina, Seattle all called. Most importantly, the man who would change my life called, the sweetest man you ever wanted to meet: Daddy Vince.

I'm talking about Vince McMahon Sr., who I became fast friends with and who I would go on to call Daddy Vince. I started working for Daddy Vince in 1955. Did you ever meet somebody and you just felt instantly like you've known him your whole life and that he just belongs there? That's the way I felt about Vince from the get-go.

The name of Daddy Vince's company was Capitol Wrestling, and he had an office in Washington, D.C., and one in New York. He

and his wife, Juanita, had a home in Fort Lauderdale at the time. He controlled Baltimore, New York, and New Jersey, and he was starting to become the biggest promoter around.

The thing about Daddy Vince was that he was absolutely fair about everything. He was just so sweet, so good to everybody. The same can be said today about Vince Jr., which is why everybody who doesn't work for him wishes that they did. Yessir, a lot of his daddy rubbed off on Vince Jr. Vinny always asks me, "What do you think Dad would say about all this?" I know what he's talking about: all the glitz, all the sex, the wacky plots.

"Well, he'd probably be real upset at first," I'd say. "But only at first. Because then he'd realize you've just adjusted to the times, that's all."

Daddy Vince was a very gentle man, and you'd be surprised to know that his son is just as sweet. When I was stuck in that hospital in late 2000, one of the first things the nurse told me when I finally came to was "Your boss called every single day." The next day the phone rang. "Hi, Lil, it's Vince," he said, and that made my whole day right there. Over the years, I've seen him help so many people without calling attention to himself. People who are down-and-out, he'll give them chances to straighten up, even though a lot of times they'll still be buttholes and pull the same crap all over again. But Vince doesn't give up, and he goes about helping people quietly. The best thing I can say about him is that his daddy would be proud.

Don't get me wrong, Daddy Vince had an Irish temper, too, just like Vinny. He didn't take no crap, but he didn't dish it out, either. Thinking back now on the few times I saw Daddy Vince blow his stack, I know where Vinny gets his passion from.

One thing both men had in common was that your relationship with them was more than business. You really are treated like you're part of the McMahon family. Promoters from all over the country started calling me, trying to book me. But Daddy Vince became more than just a promoter; he was kind of like my agent. Every time someone called with a possible booking, I'd call Daddy Vince and tell him who called and ask if I should go and how much I should ask for.

He became a close personal friend. There were so many times he'd go out of his way for little ol' me, that they're too numerous to mention.

One night stands out in my memory. It was much later—1973, to be exact. It was my birthday, but I hadn't told anyone that. I was in New York on this particular night to do a job and was concentrating on my match against Vicki Williams. Now, Vicki had never beaten me and I wasn't about to let her break that streak on my birthday. (Don't go wondering how old I was turning that night, figuring you can then do the math and come up with how old I am now. I told you, it's unladylike to give out one's age.)

I remember that match clearly. Vicki had me in a headlock early, but I grabbed a fistful of her blond hair and threw her over my shoulder. She landed on her back and I swiftly kicked her in the head. Poor girl, she was dazed as I pulled her to her feet and smacked her in the jaw. Now, remember, I'm a sweet, merciful person—out of the ring. Inside, well, that's another matter. So I got Vicki in an armlock around her neck and began to strangle her,

while gouging out her left eye at the same time. Hey, all's fair in love and war, right?

Somehow, Vicki broke free and the dropkicks started coming. She was a good athlete and her flying dropkicks were always a thing of beauty. She turned the momentum around on me, so I went back to a tried-and-true strategy. I led her to believe she had me on the ropes. I started pleading for mercy, my hands in front of my face, even offering her my hand, kind of like to pledge not to play dirty. By now, the crowd was going crazy, telling Vicki not to trust me. Smart crowd. She reached out to take my hand, and that was all she wrote. Before she knew what hit her, her shoulders were pinned for a count of one-two-three and the match was over.

But what I remember most from that night followed the match. Daddy Vince invited me to Jimmy Weston's Supper Club on East Fifty-fourth Street, a fancy place where the men all dressed in suits and the ladies wore sparkling diamonds. Out in front of the restaurant was a long line of black limousines, Caddies, Continentals, some Mercedeses. Inside, Daddy Vince was at a big table, and his eyes lit up when he saw me. "Great show tonight, Lil," he called, introducing me around the table. They made room for me next to Vinny, who everyone called Junior back then. He was already showing signs of the great businessman he'd become, because he wouldn't stop talking about Evel Knievel's upcoming Snake River Canyon jump, which he owned the closed-circuit television rights to. I'll never forget what happened after we ate; the waiter put down a cake in front of me and, suddenly, everyone was singing "Happy Birthday." I couldn't help myself, I started to cry, thinking how lucky I was to have had the McMahons so warmly take me into their own family. Believe me, there are plenty of wrestlers who go their entire lifetimes and never get treated so nicely by their promoters, instead always feeling like they're being taken advantage of.

I never felt that way with Daddy Vince. Back in 1955, he was the first one to put wrestling on TV. It was every Wednesday night in Washington, D.C., in a beat-up old barn just off Sixteenth Street. On winter nights, it was so cold that you'd be in the ring, wearing your modest outfit, and you'd look out at an audience where everybody was shivering in their parkas. In the summer, it was so hot you'd be dripping sweat before you even stepped foot in the ring.

I used to get in my car and drive from Columbia to Washington and do a two-out-of-three falls match on television and then turn around and drive straight home. Now, normally when you wrestled for Daddy Vince, you got paid real well, because he was one of the first to split the gate proceeds with the wrestlers. But on TV nights, you got a flat twenty-five-dollar fee. Some of the wrestlers would complain that we only got twenty-five dollars for such hard work, but not me. That's because Daddy Vince and I were on the same page; we both sensed that this TV thing was going to be big and that this once-a-week show was a way for us to get big, too. It was

like advertising. I appreciated him wanting me to be on his show, because I knew that if the people didn't know who you were, they weren't going to pay to see you. And I believed Daddy Vince when he said that in the future, the way to get known was to be on the TV.

The interviews that took place beforehand on a makeshift stage in front of the ring were just as important as matches. People would come early to hear and see the interviews that would be used throughout the television show, so I started trying to be wild and crazy, and entertain the crowd. I'm convinced that the interviews became more popular than the actual wrestling. Once, I broke my arm in a match against Betty Boucher, another girl I trained, but I still drove all that way just to be interviewed for the TV broadcast.

And it paid off quickly, too. I started taking the wrestling world by storm. I was wrestling about three times a week, and it seemed like every night the crowds got bigger and bigger. And more and more people became interested in coming to see this arrogant, bitchy Slave Girl Moolah get hers.

Meantime, June Byers—you remember her from my Billy Wolfe days—held the Women's Championship. But June got a crazy idea in her head. She announced she was retiring with the championship. She thought she could just retire as the champ and be the champ forever. Well, she had another thing coming. The Baltimore Athletic Commission stripped her of her championship and announced that there would be a Battle Royal to fill the vacated championship.

So in September 1956, thirteen girls got in the ring and had at it in a Battle Royal. Mae Young was one of them—she was feeling no pain that night. Judy Grable, too. There was girls from all over—from Texas, Ohio, and Florida. The way it worked was, if you were thrown out of the ring, that was it—you were out. And the last two standing would then go at it for the championship.

Well, it came down to me and my friend Judy Grable. Like I said before, she was a shy, naive, good girl out of the ring. But inside the ring, she had some talent. They called her the "acrobatic blonde with the educated flying feet." They called me a lot worse than that, never mind that I'd taught Judy a lot of those flying moves.

When it came down to her and me, I knew the championship would be mine. Not that Judy wasn't good; it's just that when it comes down to teacher versus student, the teacher usually comes out on top. The auditorium was packed and they were loud in their support for Judy, who didn't fight dirty. That didn't bother me none. I got a handful of that blond hair and started flipping her. See, Judy was good in a wide-open fight, but she needed room to do her drop-kicks. I figured to crowd her, to cut the size of the ring down. She got in a couple of dropkicks, but I kept working my way back inside to get her in some holds she couldn't get out of. After twelve minutes, I rolled her onto her back, covered her, and the referee took what felt like an eternity to pound out one-two-three on the canvas.

The bell rang and I was the champion.

People came streaming into the ring, presenting me with flowers and the championship belt. The face of the championship belt was blank, but the next day they'd put a picture of me in there. The crowd that had been against me was now cheering, and suddenly a microphone was put in front of me. I was scared to death. "I just want to thank everybody," I managed to say, in a tiny voice that must have had the fans wondering if that sweet voice could possibly belong to this bitchy wrestler.

I was stunned. In the dressing room, I hugged Daddy Vince as Commissioner Marshall of the athletic commission came over to congratulate me. "Vince, I don't know about this name Slave Girl," he said. "That don't sound right for somebody who is now the World Champion."

Slave Girl was just something left over from my days with Jack Pfeffer. I didn't care about it one way or the other. In fact, I hadn't given it much thought. "Well, what would you suggest?" Vince asked.

"I don't know," the commissioner said, scratching his head. "But I think it should be changed. I mean, she should still be Moolah, but we should add something else. Let's both think about it. Meantime, Moolah, congratulations. The way I look at it, anybody who is a winner over twelve girls in one night is really fabulous."

There was a pause and then Daddy Vince's eyes lit up. "That's it!" he shouted. "Let's call her the Fabulous Moolah!"

That sounded pretty good, I thought.

By the time I finished signing autographs at the auditorium that night, I was dead tired. I went back to the hotel. I'm sure Mae and some of the others were down in the hotel bar, raising hell as usual. But I had no time for that.

I celebrated the best way I knew how. I went up to my room and said my prayers, like I do every night. I thanked God for giving me the talent and the courage to make my dream come true. And I fell into a deep sleep while thinking about my daddy and that scrawny ten-year-old girl he used to take to the wrestling shows every Tuesday night after my dear mama passed on. Up there in heaven, I thought, I bet they were together, looking down, proud of their little girl. I don't know for sure, but I suspect I slept with a smile on my face all night long.

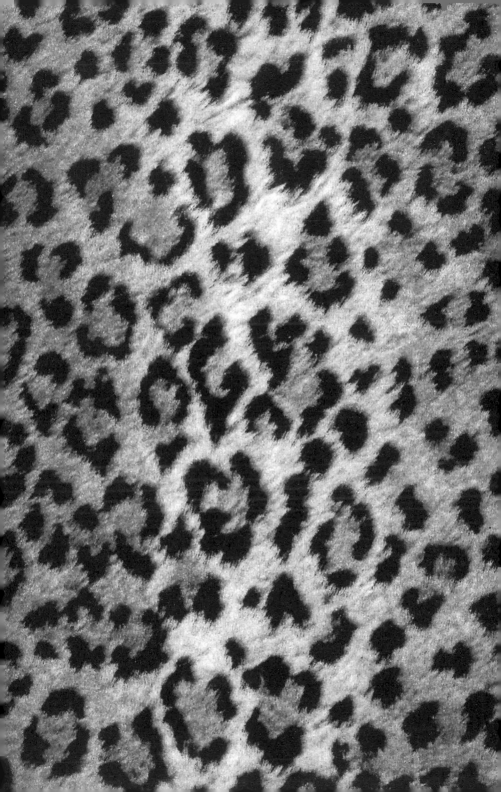

7

NEVER A DULL MOMENT

I'LL TELL YA ONE THING STRAIGHT OUT, DARLIN'. Ain't
nothing like being the best in the world at what you do. And that's
what I was. I don't say this to brag or to sound conceited, I say it
'cause it's just a plain and simple fact now as I look back on it.
Because of Billy Wolfe and the remaining power of the NWA, there
were some who didn't recognize me as the new champ right away,
but it soon became clear enough. Starting that night in 1956, I held
that championship for twenty-eight years. You can look that up.

I saw girls come and go. Each time one came out to take me on,
she was supposed to be the toughest, baddest babe to step foot in
the ring. And every single time she left the ring with my footprint
on her behind.

See, once I got that championship, I didn't stop working. If
anything, I worked harder, because I knew the girls would be gun-
ning for me. I spent extra time in the gym and practicing moves in

the ring, because I knew I'd always have to stay one step ahead of the competition. If there's one thing I know, it's that anyone who is not afraid to work has a leg up in life. That's a lesson I learned as a little girl, when I was picking cotton in the hot sun because I didn't want my daddy buying my school clothes. Throughout my life, I've always worked hard, and I've always gotten what I wanted. That's not an accident; those two things—working hard and achieving your goals—go hand in hand.

And my goal was not just to become the champion, but to stay at the top. After all, that's what Mildred Burke did, and I wanted to dominate just like she had done.

It wasn't long before I had my first real test. After I won the championship, wouldn't you know that June Byers couldn't stand just to sit on the sidelines and watch me wear that championship belt. Looking back on it, I guess I can understand how she felt. It must have been like how I felt that night in 1999 when Ivory came into the ring wearing the championship belt that I felt belonged to me.

So June came out of retirement and was making like she was going to win back the championship. Remember, June and I had a history. She gave me a pretty good butt kicking the first time I ever wrestled; we hadn't squared off against each other since then, except for during a tag-team match. June and her partner ended up winning that one, but I did pretty well against her during the times we were in the ring one-on-one.

So there I was in Louisville, defending my championship against June. She was a cocky one, all right. Going on and on about how it was her championship and the only reason I got it was because she retired. I didn't say anything—just let her run her mouth. I was younger and more fit, so I decided to use that to my advantage. I came at her as soon as the bell rang, not giving her any time to relax and settle into the match. I've always liked to be the aggressor. There are some wrestlers who are better at countering, who spin out of moves and turn the tables on their opponents. I do that, too, but what I really like is to come out full force because it sends a message: *You got a problem, sister, 'cause I'm gonna be up in your face all night long.* It's kind of intimidating and a shock to the system; sometimes the other girl just doesn't know what to do about this crazy person all up in her business.

I think that's what happened to June that night. The bell rang, and she instantly knew that she had her hands full. Around the time I smashed her face into the turnbuckle, I knew I had her. I barely broke a sweat. See, a little part of me—a very tiny part—might have been doubting that I really and truly deserved the championship. I didn't take it from her; it was awarded to me after she'd given it up on her own. So, I had two choices: I could either go on and learn to live with that little bit of doubt inside, or I could smash that doubt to smithereens by beating June to a pulp. I was extra-motivated, because I had something to prove to that little voice in-

side my head that, just every now and then, wondered if I really was ready to be wrestling's prime-time lady.

And prove it I did. June went down twice; the second time, it was for the count. That night was almost as special as the night I first won the championship, because it felt like both were somehow connected. I realized that I hadn't really won it all until I took care of June.

From then on, it seems like I was defending my championship every other night. Buddy and I were on a roll, living the good life. Between having fun with him and rolling out on the road to keep my championship, life was pretty hectic. But, still, there were moments when I'd stop and smile when I realized that on any given night inside any given arena, there might be a little girl looking up to me with wide, innocent eyes, just as I looked up at Mildred Burke all those years ago. That was a nice feeling, to think that I could maybe inspire some little girl to put aside what everybody else says and go after her dreams. I also pledged to myself that I wouldn't become all stuck-up, like Mildred had. If a kid wanted to meet me, we'd meet—and we'd talk. I was determined to treat the fans like I wanted to be treated when I was just a fan. To this day, I think that's why fans love me so much out of the ring, even while they boo me inside it.

Meantime, Buddy and I were riding high. Buddy was always a Cadillac man, and I could finally upgrade from a Chevy to a Caddy. We used to like to drive into New York and go to fancy nightclubs like the Latin Quarter and the Copacabana. We'd get a drink, and sooner or later Buddy would lead me onto the dance floor. Oh, he could cut a rug, that Buddy Lee. Back in Columbia, we'd have some killer jam sessions at the house with me on bass fiddle or guitar. Buddy didn't play an instrument; heck, he could barely play a jukebox, but he loved having musicians over, dancing and having a few drinks. Why, we'd turn our living room into a scene right out of a New York nightclub!

We were really doing well, to the point that we had pretty much put old Billy Wolfe out of business. He had the same old girls, and we were developing new faces with new and different styles, plus, I was teaching these new girls how to wrestle, something Billy had never done.

We called ourselves Girl Wrestling Enterprises, and promoters started dealing with us because they knew if I gave my word, they could bank on it. I can't tell you how often it happened that a promoter would call and say, "I need four girls for tomorrow night."

I'd book it, and they'd say, "How do you know they're going to be there?"

"Well, if one happens to get hurt and she can't make it," I'd answer, "I'll come in her place if I have to." That was enough to sell them. Over time, I got that reputation. When I said I was going to do something, it got done. That's how I've always been. Whatever I say, I do, and if I can't, I make sure they know I'm unable to meet my commitment in plenty of time. If I'm supposed to meet you at

6 P.M., and I know at 5 P.M. that something has happened, I'll call and let you know at five, so you can make other arrangements.

Girls were coming from everywhere, just showing up on my doorstep and saying they wanted to learn how to wrestle. So I'd take them in and put them up. They knew that if they stuck with it and got real good, I'd get them some bookings and send them out on the road, sometimes on my very own championship defense cards.

But being in the Girl Wrestling Enterprises stable sure wasn't easy. I was pretty hard on the girls who came through. I made a lot of demands outside of the ring. I taught them to have their hair done and their makeup on, to dress like a lady in and out of arenas. And I didn't want them hanging around in bars and dating guys in bars, because most of the guys in those bars back then were married and they had wives at home.

"If you come here to wrestle," I'd tell them, "I want you to eat, live, sleep, and drink wrestling. If you're not going to do that, go on home now." A few did up and leave, which I saw as just weeding out the girls who weren't dedicated. You can't go out to a bar and drink and dance all night long, then get up the next day, get to a booking, and put on a good show. When I'd get word that a girl was doing that, I'd have no choice but to fire her.

As far as wrestling goes, I taught the girls classic wrestling. I taught them how to fall, how to maneuver into and out of holds, the correct way to punch and take a punch. Basically, I'd teach them everything they needed to know to wrestle, from flying tactics like the dropkick and the head scissors to how to talk on the microphone in the ring and on interviews. The mistake too many wrestlers make is in thinking that interviews are just about answering questions. Instead, interviews are really about selling your character; the more outrageous you are, the better. The goal is to provide the people some entertainment and get the crowd all juiced up.

Of course, there were some things I didn't share too readily—I still had to beat some of these up-and-comers. The Moolah Whip, for instance: That's where I grab a chunk of hair and whip the other girl through the air by it. I tried to downplay that move, seeing as how I'd probably need it in some upcoming matches. I didn't want all the girls I wrestled to go and cut their hair real short!

Still, I was dedicated to my girls. I used to stress to them the importance of respecting their opponents. I told them never to blame an opponent for what happens in that ring, because it takes two to tango. On the wall in my gym in Columbia, there's a sign that says IF YOU CAN'T WIN, YOU CAN'T LOSE. IF YOU CAN'T LOSE, YOU CAN'T WIN. That's the way it goes, too. If you're not a good loser, you can't be a good winner. Because there's no way that you can win every time. Look at me, even—my run ended after twenty-eight years. (Although I still say I didn't lose that night in 1984 against Wendi Richter; I wasn't pinned because I had the pin hold on her. But we'll open that can of worms later on.)

Over the years, I taught just about every big name in women's wrestling, including Wendi Richter and Sherri Martel, both of whom you'll hear a lot about. I also taught Leilani Kai and Vicki Williams, not to mention my midgets. I love the midgets; first and foremost, my damned midget Katie.

In 1961, I was wrestling in Richmond, Virginia. On the afternoon of my show, there was a knock at my motel door. I opened the door and there was nobody standing there. Then my eyes looked down. There stood the cutest damn midget you ever saw. She had a little eighteen-inch waist and weighed all of eighty-seven pounds.

"Can I help you?" I asked.

"I want to wrestle," she barked, in a loud, demanding voice.

"You do?" I said.

"Yeah," she said. "I want to be just like you."

Now remember, hearing something like that touches me in a special place, seeing as how I pledged to myself that I'd never forget what it is to have a dream and an idol.

"Well, I don't know if you can be just like me or not," I said. "It's an awful lot of work."

"Work don't scare me," she barked again. She was an aggressive little thing, but I could tell that her bark was covering up a sweetness.

"How old are you?" I asked.

"I'm seventeen," she said.

"Well, you have to be eighteen, or get me a permission slip notarized by your parents," I told her.

Well, talk about persistence. Not fifteen minutes had gone by when there was another knock at my door. Again I opened it and found no one to be there. Until I looked down. There was Katie again.

"My mother's outside," she said, grabbing my hand and leading me to her.

Katie's mom wasn't a little person, though she wasn't too big, either. I tried making small talk—so to speak—but she was all business. "I'll sign a permission slip," she said. "She's been driving me crazy about doing this wrestling thing."

I told her she could send her daughter to me in Columbia, provided she brought the permission slip and we agreed that if Katie got hurt I wouldn't be responsible. She said they would, but I couldn't be sure this wasn't just some seventeen-year-old midget's passing fancy.

A week later, back in Columbia, my phone rang. "Hello, Moolah, this is Katie," a voice called out.

"Who?"

"Don't you remember? Katie, from Richmond," she said. "I'm in Columbia, at the Greyhound bus station." Lucky for her I was home; no one had ever called to tell me she was coming!

I went and picked her up. When she got in the car, she opened

her purse and pulled out a cigarette. In her tiny hands, it looked like the longest cigarette known to mankind. She lit it and looked up at me. "Hey," she said, "can I call you Ma?"

"No, ma'am," I said. "Anybody that smokes cannot call me Ma."

"Oh yeah?" she said.

"That's right."

She sat there for a moment, took a long puff on the cigarette, and rolled down her window. She got the pack out of her purse and threw the cigarette, followed by the whole pack, out the window.

"Now can I call you Ma?" she asked.

"Well," I said, "how long is that going to last?"

"Forever. I'll never smoke again."

"All right," I said. "If you never smoke again, you can call me Ma."

Ever since, Katie has been calling me Ma or Mom, and she never smoked again. I like to tell her that I saved her life—if I hadn't stopped her from smoking, she might have gotten cancer.

It sure has been a special friendship between Katie and me. She was there with me through all the fun in the 1960s with Buddy, and she was a friend whose shoulder I could cry on when things with Buddy started to go bad.

A lot of the girls who I trained used to get mad at me because I wouldn't let them date boys who were in our business. It's funny, how I came to see that old Jack Pfeffer's instinct was right. I learned from experience that it wasn't a good mix, two wrestlers trying to share a personal life at the same time. The reason was that Buddy's career in the ring wasn't really doing too well in the sixties. I think Jack made a mistake trying to turn Buddy into the next Buddy Rogers. That's putting too much pressure on somebody, because there would never be another Buddy Rogers, not really. Besides, Buddy might have looked like Buddy Rogers, but he didn't have his sense of style in the ring, that knack for ring showmanship I'm always talking about.

So as my career took off, as I got bigger and better bookings, and larger and wilder crowds, Buddy seemed to become a bit jealous. When he and I were booked on the same card, I was the top act. And he was the opening act.

I don't know too many men who would have liked that situation, let alone an Italian man. Buddy was very proud, and he believed a man is superior to a woman, so he was having real difficulty with the fact that I was more famous and successful than him.

I tried to talk to him about it. At the time, we had thirty-two girls that we were training and booking. I said, "Do you want me to retire and stop? I could just stay home and train the girls we've got."

Now, as you know by now, that was a big offer on my part. To this day, I wonder if I could have followed through with giving up the road for the sake of my marriage. But Buddy was torn. I could tell he didn't like the way things were going, but he didn't want me to give up all I was getting. "Why should you stop now?" he said. "You're making good money. You can't stop."

"Why don't you retire, and that way there will be no more friction?" I asked. That didn't fly, either.

So into the late sixties, things just kept going on as they had been—tense—with me bringing in the money and Buddy staying home more and keeping the school running. Around this time, an eighteen-year-old girl by the name of Rita Cortez came to us. Her mother brought her by; she wanted to be a wrestler.

Rita was a dark-skinned Mexican girl, and I just loved her to death. I thought of her as a little angel. Like a lot of the girls, she had idolized me and kind of wanted to be me. She was always trying to help me around the house, and I took her under my wing like she was a daughter or sister.

Whenever I would go shopping for myself, if I bought myself a pair of panties and a bra, I'd buy Rita the same. In my mind, by treating her so well, I was making up for how cold Mildred Burke had been to me all those years before.

At that time in Columbia, there was a lot of racial stuff going on. I never did understand why people judged the sweetness of others' souls by the color of their skin, and that kind of thinking used to get me really mad. But I'd never give in to it. For instance, because she was so dark, people used to mistake Rita for being black. Well, I'd take her downtown to the movies—she loved the movies— but I'd always get into a fight with the cashier to allow Rita to sit downstairs with the white people. The cashier would think she was black, and the blacks back then had to sit up in the balcony. This was when segregation was in full force.

"No, she's not black, she's Mexican," I'd say. "And she's sitting with me."

Sometimes the movie-house management wouldn't give in. "Look at me," I'd say. "What color am I?"

"White."

"Well, this is my daughter," I said. "She's got some dark blood in her, but if she's my daughter and you say I'm white, isn't she white, too?"

Usually, because people in Columbia knew me, they'd let Rita sit with me, though she didn't like it when I made a scene. "It's okay, I'll sit upstairs," she'd whisper. But I wasn't about to stand for such a stupid rule.

Now, I mentioned that Rita tried to do everything like me. We got a complaint to that effect from Jim Crockett, a big promoter in the Carolinas. He called Buddy after Rita did one of his shows.

"Listen, Buddy, when I want Moolah, I don't need Rita Cortez," he said.

"What do you mean?"

"Rita's match here last night," Crockett explained. "She tried to do everything Moolah does, every move, every gesture. I don't want that. My audiences don't want to see someone imitating Moolah. I'll pay Moolah to come if I want Moolah."

Crockett warned Buddy that he didn't want Rita imitating me in any of his arenas ever again. I must admit, I was kind of flattered that Rita was copying my style that much, but she was also going a bit overboard. I guess Crockett's call should have sent off warning signals, but I didn't think much of it again until one of my other girls called me while I was on the road in Houston. She was very upset.

This girl knew what a grind the road was and she knew that every dime I was making, save my expenses, I was sending home to Buddy. It sounded like she was crying. "Lillian," she said. "You work too hard for what they're doing to you."

I was confused, but at the same time a knot formed in the pit of my stomach. "What who's doing to me?"

She paused. "Rita and Buddy," she said. Turns out, she says, they'd been stepping out for quite some time when I'd been on the road.

I decided to make an unexpected trip home. The whole way, I was going back and forth in my mind, between believing and not believing what I'd been told. One thing that was starting to make sense to me was the way that Rita did every single thing just like me. One minute I'd think, *Maybe that was her way of getting her hooks into Buddy, by making herself a younger me, one that was around to pay him attention, too.* The next minute I'd feel ashamed for thinking that either one of them would do something like this to me. Then again, I'd think back on the fact that I'd been sending all this money home, and then I'd get back there and it would all be gone. Could he be spending it on her? I wondered. And then I'd turn right back around and wonder how I could be such an awfully suspicious person, and I'd feel bad.

Well, there was no more doubt when I walked in my house that day. Let's just say that what I saw left little to the imagination. I just stood there, looking at this scene, my blood boiling. And if it wasn't

Lillian Ellison

for what happened next, I probably would have ended up doing something that got me hauled off to jail for a long, long time. I'm not one who ever went in for all that wacky "other world" stuff before, but thank God, right when I was standing there stewing in all that rage, a vision of my mother appeared before me. "Lillian," she said, in a soothing voice. "It's not worth it. Turn around and leave."

I did as Mama said, but I looked back when I opened the door. "Get your things and get Rita's things and get out of my house," I said. " 'Cause if you're here when I get back, they're gonna carry you out of here in a bag." Rita actually wound up staying with Buddy for the rest of her life.

Boy, that was a tough time. Like I told you, Buddy could be so sweet, and he kept trying to get back in my good graces. But once something like that happens, it's no use to try again because you're always going to have it in your head and you'll never get along just right.

So that was the end of that. Buddy was angry that I wouldn't take him back. We had about four carloads of girls out on the road at the time, and Buddy had the cars picked up. The girls were all loyal to me, though, so he ended up taking the cars and I kept the girls. He and Rita tried to run their own wrestling organization, but that didn't work out.

Eventually, Buddy made his way to Nashville. I think he wanted to hurt my feelings because the next thing he did was hook up with

Audrey Williams, Hank's former wife. Talk about things coming around, full circle. You know, Buddy was a real charmer, a good salesman. Audrey had a country-music booking agency at the time, and they formed a partnership together. They moved to Atlanta and opened the Audrey/Lee Booking Agency.

Pretty funny, how life works, huh? Audrey ended up committing suicide and Buddy started managing Hank Williams Jr.'s career round about the mid-seventies. Somehow, Buddy and I started becoming close again.

I don't know what it was about the two of us, but we were drawn to each other, even after so much pain. Buddy would be on the road with Hank, and I'd be on the road wrestling; he'd call me at all hours, and we'd talk through the lonely nights. I'd be in some hotel room somewhere and he'd be on the tour bus, and he'd call.

"Buddy, I got to go to sleep," I remember saying to him, time and again, as I lay there in the dark, his voice in my ear; sometimes I'd fall asleep and he'd still be talking.

"Honey, you hear me?" he'd say, startling me awake. "You hear me?"

"Of course," I'd mumble, half asleep.

Things turned bad between Buddy and Hank; Hank didn't get all the money he thought he had coming to him and he sued Buddy. I was the friend Buddy turned to when he was down-and-out.

It meant a lot, after all we'd been through together, to be there for him, just to listen on those late-night phone calls.

About four years ago Buddy called and told me, "You know I've always loved you, and I always will—even after I'm gone." He had cancer. He passed away on Valentine's Day 1999.

The next day my friend Micki, who was away on vacation, asked me to drive past her house just to check on it. Katie and I got in the car and made our way over. On the way back, we took a back road. We were both upset over Buddy's passing, so we weren't saying much. The radio was playing low as we passed by an old church on this gravelly country road.

Now, what happened next sounds crazy, but it happened. There was a loud swooshing sound as a big white cloud came flying straight for our windshield. I jammed on the brakes and reached out with my right hand to hold Katie, because she wasn't wearing her seat belt. That cloud stood still in the air right in front of us and, just for an instant, took form; I swear to God it was Buddy's face. It was just the face, and then the cloud tapered off like a cone. But Buddy was right there, kind of grinning sideways like he used to, and he said something to us, something like "I'm okay" or "I'm happy." And then, just like that, he was gone, and there we were in the middle of a dirt road, silent, our hearts beating a mile a minute.

We drove on a few blocks before I looked over at Katie. "You okay?" I asked.

"Yeah, Mom."

"Did you see what I saw, darlin'?"

"I believe I did," Katie said. "Did you see what I saw?"

"What did you see?" I asked.

And then she said, "Buddy."

We didn't say another word until we pulled into our driveway. Katie looked at me. "Mom, if I hadn't been with you, I would have never believed it," she said.

"Katie, I wouldn't have told you, because I know you wouldn't have believed it."

I got to say, after I dealt with the shock of it, I was comforted by that vision. It was just like Buddy to tell me he was okay, and to show me that cockeyed grin of his one last time. Despite all our problems, I really do believe he was a sweet man and my one true love. We had a lot of fun, and we had a lot of fights. But there was never a dull moment, and if you snapped your fingers and offered me the chance to redo all those years with Buddy, guess what? I wouldn't change a damned thing.

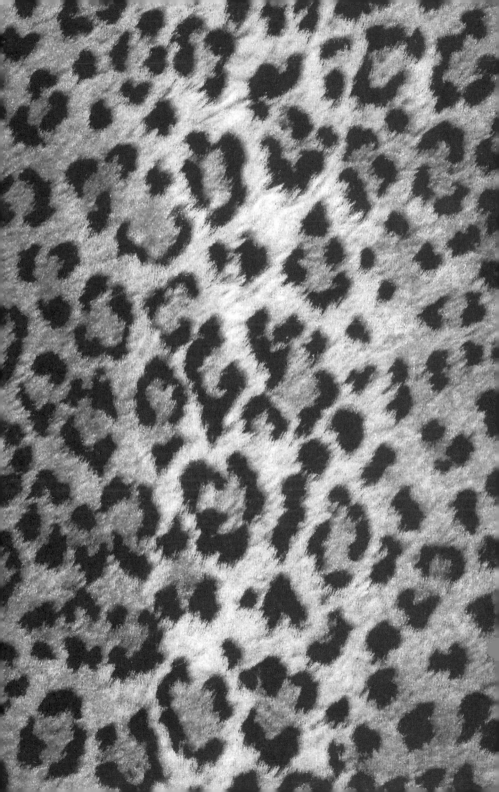

8

Making History

S THE 1970S GOT UNDER WAY, it became clear I was a different kind of champion. Mildred Burke and June Byers had both been popular with fans not only because they won but because they played it wholesome. In terms of their ring characters, they were both good girls.

Well, I had learned that you can entertain people a whole lot better by being bad. You know by now that if nothing else, I tell it like it is. I'm a straight shooter, darlin', and I let the chips fall where they may. So how's this for not trying to run away from the way things happened: I have no qualms whatsoever telling you, I was a dirty wrestler. And the fans loved it.

I used to like to take a weapon, a piece of pipe for instance, into the ring with me. I'd hide it in my tights and check to see when the referee wasn't looking; then I'd take the weapon out and introduce it to my opponent, usually across the head, while shielding the ref's view with my body. The crowd would start screaming and booing, but suddenly they'd be preoccupied about whether or not I was going to get caught. It was a way for the fans to be involved in the outcome, too, because they'd come running up to the ring, screaming at the referee, "She's got a pipe! Are you blind?" When that happened, of course, the referee would look over at them, giving me another great chance to pull the weapon from my tights and use it right quick to open a gash on the poor girl grappling with me.

This would go on for quite a while. Sometimes, I'd even let my opponent steal the weapon away from me, but only if the time was right—that is, right before the referee looked over. That way, he'd discover it in *her* possession and disqualify *her*! I used to love it when that happened, because the fans would all get crazy. Just to rub their noses in it, I'd waltz around the ring, showing off my championship belt and once in a while holding up the pipe, too, which never failed to get a big reaction from the crowd.

What I had learned, of course, is that people love a villain. I would have been bored to tears if the character I played in the ring was always some Goody Two-shoes. There is a difference between being a bit bad and being evil, and I never crossed that line. I was bad, and people liked that, because people who are a little bad, a little flawed, are more interesting than people who have no dark side whatsoever to their personalities. I've been proven right, too, if you look at wrestling nowadays. You needn't look any further than one of my favorites, Stone Cold Steve Austin, who has many of these same qualities.

Around this time I developed a favorite finishing move or two. I'd get myself trapped in a corner and my opponent would come charging at me, shoulder first. Then she'd follow up with a hard knee. I'd make it look like I could barely stand. Then, suddenly, as the girl came back in for a shoulder block, I'd dodge it, spin her around, and before she knew what hit her, I'd pick her up under the crotch with one hand. I'd hold her high in the air, where she'd be helpless, and the crowd would roar, anticipating a body slam.

Far be it from me to disappoint the fans. But rather than just a run-of-the-mill body slam, I'd throw that girl down while I lowered myself and stuck out one knee. Her back would land across my knee: a backbreaker. She'd roll off my knee and be spread-eagle on the canvas on her back. All I'd have to do is cover her to get a three-count from the ref. But that would lack style. So what I'd do is pin the girl by folding her body into a small package. I'd pin her shoulders under her own body weight, with her butt high in the air and her boots touching the canvas right on either side of her own head.

You would think that would be it. But you'd be wrong. The ref would give the three-count, but I'd always want to leave the crowd and the girl I was wrestling something to remember Moolah by. So

after the bell rang, I'd land either a hard chop or a solid kick smack-dab to the center of the girl's chest. Boy, that would get the crowd worked up—a cheap shot after the bell!

Remember what I was saying about intimidating your opponent? Well, nothing sent a better intimidating message for next time—after all, I was wrestling a lot of the same girls every other week—than forcing your opponent to walk off through the crowd with a giant red imprint of your hand or boot on her chest. That's what I used to like to call my Moolah Brand. I remember doing just that once to my good friend Donna Christantello, another girl I taught. After my finishing move, I laid her out with a chop to the chest that echoed throughout the arena like a grenade exploding. I can still hear the crowd gasping and laughing while I watched Donna walk off with that big red spot throbbing on her chest. Give her credit, though, because she wouldn't give me the satisfaction of seeing her touch it as she made her way to the dressing room, even though it must have stung something fierce.

After you'd seen these kinds of wrestling matches, there is no way you could come away thinking that women weren't meant to wrestle. It wasn't just me who was hard-nosed, tough as nails, and athletic to boot. To some degree or another it was every single one of the girls. I had seen boxing matches where big guys would dance around the ring and do everything they could to avoid fighting. You've seen those, right? They spend all this time moving around the ring, throwing a phantom punch here and there, and really what they're doing is stalling for time because they don't really want to mix it up.

Well, you didn't see none of that in women's wrestling. We knew we were there to give the people what they wanted, and they wanted to see some down and dirty brawling. And that's what we gave them.

When we were allowed to, that is. See, even into the early seventies, it was illegal for women to wrestle in seven states, including, believe it or not, New York. You know by now how I react when I come up against some stupid rule. I declare war on it. And that's exactly what I did in the early seventies with that law that said women couldn't wrestle.

The New York State Athletic Commission had actually come right out and said they banned ladies' wrestling "for their own good." They thought women risked serious health problems, including getting breast cancer, by taking part in such a violent profession. As proof, they pointed to Billy Wolfe's adopted daughter, Janet Wolfe, who died in the ring that night in a tag-team match that Mae Young was a part of.

Of course, there was a long history of men dying in boxing matches, yet that was perfectly legal in New York. To his great credit, Daddy Vince took the lead in fighting to overturn this piece of discrimination.

"Moolah, is this a stupid rule or what?" I remember Daddy Vince asking me. He pointed out that we could wrestle across the river in New Jersey but not in New York. "You want to try and get this law overturned?"

I didn't miss a beat. "Hell, yes," I said, itching for a fight.

"With you leading the way, Moolah," Daddy Vince said, "I know we can do it."

Once Daddy Vince and I decided to partner on this, it became a big issue. See, most promoters didn't want to stand up to the state commissions that were still discriminating against female wrestlers. Why should they, if they were doing just fine without putting on lady wrestling shows? In other words, a lot of promoters were already getting standing-room-only crowds for their shows, so why go and try to fix something that ain't broke?

Well, that wasn't Daddy Vince's way. If he saw something that was wrong, he was damned sure going to do his level best to make it right. And by now, he had a lot of clout. He was taking wrestling to new levels. His shows were selling out the Boston Garden, the Philadelphia Spectrum, and New York City's Madison Square Garden all the time now. In fact, he put on twenty-one straight sellouts at Madison Square Garden. There were many times when he would show a closed-circuit telecast of his shows in the Felt Forum (today known as the Theatre at Madison Square Garden), right next to the Garden, for all those who tried and failed to get into the main event next door! He was doing so well, so it wasn't a business decision that made him lead this fight. No, Daddy Vince knew it was wrong to discriminate—period—and so did I.

Like I said before, I hate it when men try and tell me what I can and cannot do and then add insult to injury by telling me that they

know what's best for me. Well, every member of those athletic commissions were men, and they would look at you with a straight face and tell you they were banning you from your livelihood "for your own good." Don't do me any favors, I'd tell them.

Daddy Vince got his lawyers on the case, and I met with them and we started going to war. Everywhere I went, I issued a standard challenge: "I'm never retiring until I'm able to wrestle in Madison Square Garden," I'd say, before and after matches in packed arenas across the country. There was a magazine by the name of *Wrestling Monthly*, and its editor, Norman Kietzer, got excited by what we were doing, and he started writing editorials about the discrimination, saying the actions taken by the New York commissioners were "illegal and immoral." I'd call him up and say, "You tell 'em, Norman!"

I went to Albany and testified before some committee of men who liked to use big words that made this issue seem more complicated than it really was. I did my homework, though. A friend had given me an article that I still keep with me, entitled "The Stronger Sex." And it was all about how women—the stronger sex referred to in the title—have, truth be told, always wrestled.

So I started giving those boys a history lesson. If you looked back at Greek mythology, there was an account of how a goddess beat a young man in every kind of sport—archery, throwing the discus, javelin, and wrestling! There were also the Amazons, women known for their skills in war. There are records of women wrestlers carrying off the highest awards at the ancient Olympic Games. I remember reading a story of a Tartar princess who convinced her father that no suitor could have her unless he could outwrestle her, and as proof of his intentions, suitors had to put up a thousand ponies as collateral. Well, that princess soon owned herself ten thousand ponies, because those men couldn't beat her.

I'd invite those commissioners to my matches so they could see that girl wrestlers were just as popular as the best of the weaker sex—oops, excuse me, I mean, men. And in every interview I gave, I'd talk about how unfair it was that in the 1970s, women couldn't wrestle in some places. And it wasn't just some places—we were focusing on New York, because we figured if we could turn the tide in New York, the remaining six states (all in the Northeast) would lift their bans, too. This was the early 1970s, mind you, a time when women in New York were burning bras and calling themselves Women's Libbers. How strange is it, I'd ask, that my hometown of Columbia, South Carolina, allowed women to wrestle and this big, fancy Eastern city wouldn't?

I went up to Philadelphia to do *The Mike Douglas Show*, a nationally syndicated TV talk show. I'm convinced that my appearance on that show led to the ban finally being overturned. One of the other guests was the football player, Roosevelt Grier. He was a big bear of a man who played for the Los Angeles Rams—and he'd pop up years later

Lillian Ellison

in the O. J. Simpson murder case, when, in his role as a pastor, he went to see O. J. It was rumored that O. J. confessed to him, but Rosey could never say anything about it one way or the other, because their conversation was confidential since Rosey had become a man of the cloth.

Anyway, Rosey was on that show in Philadelphia, and I started talking about how women can do anything men can do. Not any woman, mind you, but a well-trained, dedicated woman could do just as good inside a wrestling ring as a man. Being a good wrestler isn't all about brute strength, just like boxing isn't either. If that were true, all those big football players like Ed "Too Tall" Jones and Mark Gastineau wouldn't have gotten their butts kicked when they tried to box.

Wrestling, like boxing, is about skill. I'm all of five-four, but I know how to flip a 250-pound man over my shoulder. It's about weight shift, the momentum of your body, and getting your legs behind you.

Big Rosey Grier didn't believe me. So, right there on national TV, when he reached out to shake my hand, I grabbed him and arm-drug him across the stage. Boy, was that a funny sight, this giant football player squaring off against little old me. He must have been close to three hundred pounds, and there I was, half his weight. Yet he couldn't stop me from dragging him around by the arm in front of that audience. The folks in the studio gasped and Mike Douglas swore up and down that we weren't pretending. I heard later on that

Rosey Grier walked around with a sling holding that arm for two weeks after that.

I can't believe how many people saw that show. That's all people were talking to me about before and after all of my matches. I guess those commissioners took in the show, too. In June 1972, the New York State Athletic Commission legalized women's wrestling. Daddy Vince called to tell me the good news.

"We did it, Vince!" I yelled.

"We sure did, Moolah," he said. "And guess what? You're finally going to get your dream—to wrestle in Madison Square Garden. You have to be the first lady wrestler to do that, and it'll be a championship defense!"

"Tell me when and I'm there," I said.

Well, it was July 1, 1972, and I'll never forget hearing the hum of the crowd from my dressing room. There were 19,512 fans there; in the main event, they'd see Pedro Morales demolish George Steele, but first they'd see history made. They'd see women wrestle in the Garden.

To this day, Madison Square Garden is my favorite place to put on a show. I might not have cared much for living in New York with Buddy way back when, but when it comes to where you're going to wrestle, nowhere has more excitement than New York. They don't call that building the Mecca for nothing. When you walk from the dressing room to the floor, and hear that buzz from the crowd, you get goose bumps.

I came out wearing my championship belt, with my picture right there in the center of it. I was wearing a multicolored fringed cowgirl jacket, and I strutted into that ring while the public-address system played some good old-fashioned, kick-ass country music.

My challenger came in, and the folks offered her their encouragement. It was none other than Vicki Williams, so there'd be no surprises. Well, maybe one. When I saw her making her way into the ring, I noticed that her blond hair was cut even shorter than usual. You might think that would get me worried—now I couldn't grab a fistful of hair and swing her around. Instead, it got me even more confident, because it meant that she was frightened of me. It meant I had gotten into her head. Knowing that, plus the fact that I was so pumped to finally realize my dream of performing at Madison Square Garden, made me know I couldn't lose.

Referee Dick Kroll took my championship belt from me and called the two of us to the center of the ring. He held the championship belt up for everybody to see what we were fighting over. "There's a reason my picture's in there, girl," I said to Vicki, getting real close in her face. "It's mine."

She didn't say anything. I could tell she was nervous. When I watch sports on TV nowadays, whether it's wrestling, boxing, ten-

nis, or golf, I can almost tell from how the player is carrying him- or herself just who is going to win. When you get to the top level, there's not much that separates players in terms of skill. Instead, so much of it has to do with who is up to the pressure of the moment. And that night, with us making history in front of 19,000 fans, it was my moment. It was one I'd dreamed of. The way her legs were shaking, it looked like it was a moment Vicki had been dreading.

Vicki got a couple of good leg holds on me, but I reversed out of them. I gave the Garden fans a glimpse of some vintage Moolah. There were a few open palm slaps upside Vicki's head that had her staggering, and one body slam that I thought knocked all the air out of Vicki when I went to cover her for the pin. But she's a heckuva competitor, and she just barely got her right shoulder off the mat between counts two and three, and then kicked out.

But it was over soon after that. I trapped her by the ropes and pinned her with a quick reverse jackknife that had the crowd oohing and ahhing when the ref counted to three and the bell sounded. I held that championship belt up over my head and circled the ring, blowing kisses to the crowd, who were now cheering wildly for me.

Vince Jr. was the ring announcer back then and he hopped up into the ring.

"How about the Ladies' Champion of the world, the Fabulous Moolah!" he said, holding my arm up, as the crowd roared.

Then the fans really got excited when Vince went on to make an announcement. "Moolah has already been signed to appear in defense of her championship on the next card here at Madison Square Garden!"

I left the ring, blowing kisses to the crowd, and I could still hear the cheers in my dressing room. I had finally performed on sports' biggest stage, and I was a hit. And I couldn't wait for my next championship defense at the Garden.

9

MARRIED TO THE JOB

I'T'S NOT LIKE THERE'S ANY ONE MOMENT in time when you decide to make a decision like this. More often than not, life just happens to you, which is what happened to me in the early seventies, after all the time I spent trying to get women's wrestling legalized in New York.

At some point it just became clear to me that I was married to wrestling—and wouldn't be getting married to anybody else. I had already had three husbands, plus a couple of other romances that nearly tossed my whole world upside down. After all that happened with Buddy, I knew I was doing the best thing by just burying myself in wrestling. Don't get me wrong. If a fella wanted to date, so long as he was nice and a gentleman, I'd go out to dinner and a club or take in a show now and again. So I enjoyed myself. But my mama told me, "Stand up for your rights," and back in those days it just seemed that you had to give up too much of who you were when you decided to share your whole life with someone else.

Besides, it's not like I was all alone. My damn midget Katie was living with me, of course, and we had us a blast. Plus, my dear friend Donna Christantello lived with me, off and on, for about forty years. Donna was a heckuva wrestler and an even better friend. All these years of putting my girls up on my property, and to this day, not counting Mae, only two of them have lived in the main house with me: Katie and Donna.

They're more than friends; they're family. When Donna's mother passed away, I was the first person she called. She went back home to Pittsburgh when it happened, and I went with her, to help her take care of her family. Not long after that, she returned the favor. My oldest brother, Ed, had muscular dystrophy and he had three kids. Well, before I knew it, Donna was living in his home and taking care of his kids when he was in the hospital for the two months before he died.

She's always been like a sister to me. She lived with me until May 1999, when she moved back to Pittsburgh. We like to go to Las Vegas together, where I'm a blackjack fiend. I love to go out there for a week and just play. What I do is, I put the money that I'm going to gamble with in my purse. If I lose it, I quit. If I win, I'll keep in reserve what I brought and play with the rest. I usually come out ahead, and then Donna and I will go and have us a steak dinner for the pre–World War II prices they got there.

Donna was a darn good wrestler, too. She and Toni Rose were the tag-team champions for a while. Toni was from Terre Haute,

Indiana, and was about five-six and 135 pounds. Once I sent her to El Salvador to take part in a show where she squared off against a 150-pound male wrestler, before a crowd of three thousand crazy El Salvadorans in an arena with a capacity for just one thousand people. Well, Toni started beating her man, and the next thing you know, some of the audience were throwing lit cigarettes into the ring—and the ring caught fire. The cops rushed everybody out in a stampede, and when Toni got back to the States she told me she'd never go to El Salvador again—unless the promoter came up with a really big cash offer she couldn't refuse.

Lillian Ellison

For about eight months, Toni and I were the tag-team champs, too. But I never did go in too much for tag teams. The problem was I just didn't have enough room for all those damn championship belts. Plus, I didn't like sharing the spotlight with a tag-team partner. Remember what I told you about ring showmanship? You can't keep everybody's attention when you're just standing outside the ropes, waiting for a tag. I'm there to wrestle, not to watch the action like a fan.

Toni was a nice girl, and so was Leilani Kai. Leilani was from Florida; I gave her that name because she had a little bit of a Hawaiian look to her. She was dating Tanaka, a wrestler from Japan who was a three-time tag-team champ with Mr. Fuji. Tanaka used to throw salt into his opponents' eyes, and he later went on to play Pee-Wee Herman's butler in the movie Pee-Wee's Big Adventure. Anyway, Leilani, who was a lot younger than Tanaka, tried to tell me he was her uncle. "I wasn't born yesterday," I told her.

Joyce Grable was another of my girls who was just sweet as pie. She was from Columbus, Georgia, and she named herself Grable after her idol growing up, wrestler Judy Grable. Like Toni, Joyce never was a problem when she was living on my grounds.

The same can't be said for all the girls, though. Some of them wanted to be pretty wild, like one of Billy's blond bombshells who was seen one night, naked, riding down Main Street in Nashville on the hood of a car belonging to one of the Fargo Brothers! If you wanted to do that stuff, you didn't live on Moolah Drive, because Moolah ain't no damn madam, I'd tell them.

Don't get me wrong. I liked having fun, and I liked the girls to have fun. But good, wholesome fun. For example, I bought a big Winnebago in 1975 for when we went out on long road trips. Now, that was fun. It was like having a home on wheels, complete with its own big generator. Me and a couple of the girls liked to fish, so we'd bring our rods and gear. When we passed a stream while we were passing through Nowheresville, USA, we'd stop and take a couple of hours to see what we could reel in. And then we'd cook it up and fill our bellies before getting back on the road and driving all night long to the next show.

This one time, I got a call from promoter Emile DuPree of New Brunswick, Canada, looking for me and three girls to do two weeks' worth of shows throughout Canada. Well, Dottie Downs, Kittie Adams, Joyce Grable, and I loaded up the Winnebago and hit the road. It was autumn, and the colors of the changing leaves as we passed through Connecticut were so breathtaking we had to pull over and just sit by the side of the road and take it all in. Over the years, people have said to me, "I can't believe how much you travel, don't you hate it?" Well, goodness, no. I've seen more of this country than anyone I know, and to this very day, the beauty of America still amazes me. Darlin', there are still times when I get a certain view and have to pull over and just stare at it.

Anyway, we were having some fun as we drove through the Canadian countryside. This was deep into Canada now. Our first match was in a town called St. Stephens, and the promoter was really pleased with the show we put on there. The next morning, we piled into the Winnebago and were off to the next stop, a godforsaken town by the name of Heartland, Canada. Well, I'm driving along—I kid you not—and all of a sudden, out of nowhere, I got a sharp pain in my back, between my shoulder blades—like someone was behind me, stabbing me with a knife.

I started screaming bloody murder, because that's really what I thought it was. I thought someone had hidden in the Winnebago and was now stabbing me in the back with a sharp blade. The girls came running to me and had to convince me that I hadn't been stabbed. Luckily, Kittie was a good driver—she used to drive racing cars—and she grabbed the wheel and found us a hospital . . . or what passed for a hospital in Heartland, Canada.

They brought me into that emergency room, and I knew I was in trouble. There were no lights anywhere. Doctors and nurses walked around with flashlights. I didn't know if they were having a blackout, or if electricity just hadn't reached Heartland, Canada, yet.

A doctor examined me in the dark, and I kept yelling to the girls, "Get me outta here! We got a show to get to!" Needless to say, this is another one of those times when I was praying to God to see me through.

THE FABULOUS MOOLAH

The doctor told me I was having gallbladder problems, and they loaded me up on pills to ease the pain. As soon as it felt like the knife that had been twisting in me had stopped, I got the girls together and told them, "We got a show to do."

The doctor couldn't believe it. "You're taking your life in your hands, ma'am," he said.

I thought, *What does he know? He can't even read a piece of paper without having to shine a flashlight on it.*

So we got to the arena and there I was in the ring, taking a few bumps. Only the painkillers started wearing off, and it sure was a relief when the bell rang and the show was over. We found another emergency room—this one had lights—and I loaded up on some more pain pills.

But the next morning, things were worse. I woke up so swollen, I looked to be nine months pregnant. Now I knew I had to get home, only I came to find out that only two flights a week left from this godforsaken town—and I'd already missed one. So they admitted me to the hospital, where they wanted to perform surgery.

"Oh, no you don't," I told them. "I'm not letting anybody cut me but my doctor back in Columbia, South Carolina."

The next flight back to the States was to leave in two days. So I just had them load me up on pain medicine until it was time to go. That morning the promoter visited me in the hospital. At first I

thought, How nice of him to come see me. But then he cleared his throat and leaned down toward me.

"Moolah," the promoter said, "you can't wrestle tonight, huh?"

See, that's the kind of person you were often dealing with in this business. I was sure spoiled, because Daddy Vince—and later, his son—would never say anything like that to somebody. They wouldn't even think it. You were always a person first to them, and a wrestler second.

Anyway, I flew out of Canada and had to change planes in Boston. Well, going through a security check, I passed out. So now they rushed me to a Boston hospital and started prepping me for surgery, until I opened my mouth and let them have it. "No one is operating on me here," I said.

"But we have the finest facilities in the country," said the doctor.

"But you don't have my doctor, Dr. Pierre Laboard," I said, refusing to give consent for them to cut me open.

I can be a stubborn little Southern belle. I made them take me by ambulance back to the airport, where they put me on a plane for Columbia. Once that plane touched down, an ambulance was waiting for me.

Dr. Laboard has since passed on, but he was a sweet man. What I loved most about him was his bedside manner. I think that's so important, when a doctor knows how to make you feel confident about him. When he finally opened me up, he took one look at me and said, "I can't operate on you. You've got gangrene."

Uh-oh. That meant he had to spend a few days treating the gangrene condition. Finally, he came into my room and said, "Well, honey, are you ready for the grand opening?" He took me down to surgery and removed that stinking gallbladder.

Nowadays, I have friends who undergo surgery on their gallbladder, and they're up and around within a day or two because the procedure is done using lasers and such. But back in the mid-seventies, this was major surgery. It wasn't unheard of for someone to be laid up for two months recuperating.

When Dr. Laboard told me that, I just smiled. Well, I kind of winced, because I was still in a lot of pain. "Doc," I said, "you know Moolah. I'm not sitting around for two months."

Six weeks later I'd put on a tag-team show in Atlanta, as frisky as a wildcat. My illness made me miss a role that had been written for me in the Bill Cosby movie *Mother, Jugs & Speed*, and there was no way I'd miss my return to the ring, too.

But on the day I went in for the surgery, I didn't know what to expect in the way of recuperative time. Plus, there was another issue to deal with. My girls knew that my damn midget Katie was like a daughter to me, and she was due back from California on the very day they were cutting me open. No one had told Katie I was in the hospital until she got back, because they knew she'd miss her remaining

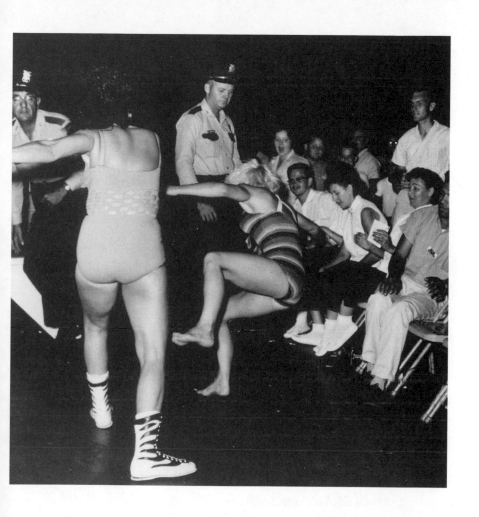

shows and take the first flight back. When she got home and heard
the news, she didn't even unpack. She cussed everybody out for keeping her in the dark and hightailed it over to the hospital, where she
put two pillows on the floor and spent the next couple of nights there
holding my hand. That's my damn midget Katie for you, yessir.

THE FABULOUS MOOLAH

Throughout much of the seventies, I kept Katie on the road, wrestling as Diamond Lil, because she was a crowd favorite. There was a promoter by the name of Jim Barnett who liked to book midget wrestling, and he had me send Katie and a few of the other tiny ones over to Australia to put on some shows. I'd always send Dick Murdoch with them, to drive them around and look out for them. This one time, Dick called from Australia, laughing hysterically.

Turns out Katie had gotten herself into a little pickle. It seems one of the other midgets was quite the little drunk. He was in the front seat with Dick, drinking a case of beer in quart bottles, which he'd toss into the backseat, right next to poor Katie, when he was done draining each one. The drunker he got, the more he kept looking Katie up and down and making lusty-type comments. Through the rearview mirror, Dick Murdoch said he could see Katie's eyes become the size of new moons rising, she was getting so mad.

Well, the little fella's drinking was getting him pretty horny, I reckon. He stood up and leaned over the front seat into the back. "I'm gonna show you what a real man looks like," he slurred, his tiny hands fiddling with his zipper.

"You better stay in that front seat and mind your own business," Katie said.

"You know you want to see a real man," he said, just about to whip it out when—*kaboom!*—Katie smashed one of those empty quarts of beer down on his little head. She knocked that midget

out, and a knot started to appear on his head that grew to be almost bigger than the rest of him. Dick pulled over at a rest stop and they laid him out on the hood of the car while they got something to eat. Wouldn't you know it, he was still out like a light when they got back! In fact, he was out and seeing stars until they finished their trip to Sydney. The next day, and from then onward, whenever this midget saw Katie approaching, he'd quickly switch to the other side of the street and keep his head down.

I still tease her about him. Just a couple of years ago, we actually saw the little guy on *The Jerry Springer Show*, doing some fool thing. I called to Katie, "Hurry up! Your honey is on the TV!"

When she saw who I was talking about, the old fume started rising again. "I could whack that damn TV off the stand!" she said.

By the mid-seventies, Katie was one of the best midget wrestlers around. Also by that time, we had all but eliminated a disease that was once taking wrestlers down pretty regularly. It was called trachoma, and it just about made you go blind. It was caused by a mixture of ring dust and sweat. One wrestler, Ed (Strangler) Lewis, nearly went blind. He couldn't tell the difference between light and darkness. It got to where he'd have to be guided to the ring, but he'd still try to put on a show, even being half-blind. The problem was that the disease was contagious; if you rubbed a used towel onto your face, you could pick it up. Heck, you could even get it from the mat during a fall. We didn't have what you'd officially call a union, but a lot of us pushed for people to pay attention to this disease. We finally all but wiped it out in the seventies, thanks to sulfate-compound treatments and injections of penicillin. But that was a scary time; with every fall, you didn't know if, by bedtime, your eyesight would be all blurry or gone.

I used to like to visit sick kids in the hospital when I was on the road. And come Sunday, no matter where I was, I always found a church to pray in. Life on the road could get pretty wild, so it felt good to check in with the Lord on Sunday and do things for those who were less fortunate. Like I said, I wasn't as wild as some of the guys and girls on the circuit, but I saw some things that convinced me never to get that out of control. Like the time when I came down to the lobby of a fancy hotel in Japan to find the son of a famous promoter, buck naked, swinging like a chimp on a vine from a crystal chandelier while swigging from a bottle of booze! "That boy's party has gone on a bit too long," I said. Then there was the famous wrestler who shall remain nameless who was known not only for his womanizing but also for one particular bedroom fetish. Seems that, after sex, he'd like to spray what he'd call a "golden shower" all over the girl. Once this got around, I never could look at him without breaking into laughter.

Anyway, by now you're getting the picture. Between the craziness of the road, training and booking my girls, fighting to wipe out trachoma, and defending my championship, I barely had time for any kind of social life. That's what I mean when I say I married

wrestling. Heck, I was so busy, it was all I could do just to stay focused enough so Vicki Williams didn't take my championship.

Throughout the seventies, Vicki was the top contender. Back then, she was a college graduate, though that doesn't always mean someone is smart; sometimes, it just means they had certain advantages in life. Anyway, Vicki was a really talented wrestler, but she could never get over that hump and beat me. Oh, but she came close a couple of times.

I remember once in Modesto, California, must have been around 1978, when she got to talking in the papers before the match. "Moolah is getting old and has held the championship for too long," she said. "I feel her time has run out."

I responded in kind. "Vicki Williams is just a spoiled brat," I said. The stage was set for another showdown.

Right out of the gate, I took control with a hammerlock, then got her in a combination of arm and wrist locks. "Give it up, Vicki," I yelled, "or I'll break your arm!"

The crowd started chanting "Go, Vicki, go!" She got free and got me good with a judo chop to the throat, followed by a trip into the turnbuckle. While she was working me over the ref asked if I was ready to concede. "Hell no!" I yelled.

Things got worse for me after that, and everyone in that arena thought they were about to witness history being made—my championship would be lost for the first time in twenty-two years. I was hung up helpless on the ropes, and Vicki charged me, ramming her blond head into my gut. She did this twice, and then I saw her coming in for another. That was her mistake. You've got to mix up your attack so you still have the element of surprise on your side, see. She put her head down as she came forward, and I took a quick step aside, like a matador dodging an oncoming bull. *Boom!* She head-butted the turnbuckle straight on. I got in a few kicks and then threw her outside the ring onto the concrete.

But by the time we got back into the ring, Vicki had recovered well enough to nail me with a couple of dropkicks and a flying leg scissors. I was pretty out of it, and things looked bleak. But again, she went to the well once too often. She came at me with another high-flying leg kick, missed, and landed all funny. As soon as I saw that not only wasn't she getting up but that she was barely conscious, I covered her for the pin, about seventeen minutes into the one-fall match.

That was as close as I came to losing to Vicki—or anyone, for that matter. At least, that is, until wrestling entered its new era in the eighties. By then, Vince Jr. had taken over for Daddy Vince and brought wrestling to new heights. But as the seventies were coming to a close, Vince Jr. was just the announcer for the matches, just another colorful character. He was always a sweet boy, but who knew he was a business genius, and that he was about to change wrestling for good?

10

ROCK, WRESTLING, AND CYNDI LAUPER

IT MIGHT HAVE TAKEN ME A LITTLE LONGER than most people, but I realized something in the early eighties that may make you laugh: It sure is good to have a few extra dollars in your pocket. Now, that may sound obvious, but the early eighties is when—thanks to Vince Jr.—wrestling really started taking off, and true to who he is, Vince started seeing to it that his performers made out really well when it came to bringing in the—you'll pardon the pun—moolah.

Remember, I didn't get started in this business to make money—I just wanted to wrestle. Sure, I took to wearing big glasses with dollar-signs on the lenses, and I owned a big dollar-sign necklace that I liked to show off to kind of play off the name Moolah. But that was me hyping the Moolah character. The truth is that money was never the most important thing to me. Which is why I stayed with wrestling through all those years of eating ketchup for breakfast,

Lillian Ellison

lunch, and dinner, of driving through the night because I couldn't afford to pay for a few hours of shut-eye in a fleabag motel.

So around about the time wrestling started to become one of the biggest means of entertainment in America, and I started seeing those bucks roll in, well, I suddenly realized: Oh, this is why everybody else has always been so hell-bent on making the almighty dollar. It's fun to have money, sugar.

The best part about it is the freedom it gives you to help your friends and loved ones. That's what truly gives me pleasure, being able to be there for all the people who were there for me when times weren't too good. Like my daughter, Mary. In 1981, Mary was looking for something to do, besides being a great mother to her six children. I had some extra money and was able to do something for Mary in the way of getting her something to do with herself.

I opened a bar and grill in Columbia called Moolah's Hideaway and told Mary that since I was on the road all the time, it could be hers and she could run it. Well, let me tell you, that turned out to be one fun place. By now, in addition to having Donna and Katie living with me in my house, I had a whole bunch of the wrestling girls living on the property. So Moolah's Hideaway was a good hangout spot for them, and it was good for me, too, because it allowed Mary to keep an eye on the girls for me when I was out of town.

Moolah's Hideaway was more than just a bar. It was very popular because I was so well known around Columbia, and it was a

place where people came to be entertained. For example, I had five midgets, including Katie, training under me and staying on the grounds at the time. So I used to dress them up as little elves as Christmas approached, and folks from all over would come to get a kick out of these little Santa's helpers.

My friend André the Giant used to love to visit Moolah's Hideaway, particularly around Christmastime, when the midgets were all done up. They'd wear those little caps and hot pants and André would come down and we'd just have a ball. André was seven-foot-four and a tad over five hundred pounds, and it was nothing for him to drink twelve or thirteen pitchers of beer himself. You'd think he was just drinking water for all the effect it had on him.

André died in 1993 of a heart attack, and I sure do miss him. He once drank 127 beers in a Reading, Pennsylvania, hotel bar, and then passed out cold in the lobby. He was so big, the staff couldn't budge him, so they threw a sheet over him and used him as lobby art until he came to. Once, he and three friends ran up a $2,700 bill at a French restaurant in New York. He and Hulk Hogan had one of wrestling's great rivalries in the eighties. At the end of the decade he'd pin Hogan for the World Wrestling Entertainment Championship, only to turn around and give the championship to Million Dollar Man Ted DiBiase, who, turned out, had paid off the referees to allow André to beat Hogan. The two also went at it at *WrestleMania III*, where Hulk pinned André in front of ninety-three

thousand fans at the Pontiac Silverdome in Michigan. This event broke the Rolling Stones' world record for the largest indoor attendance.

But that was later. Back in the early eighties, André would visit my bar because he just loved those little midgets. He'd gather all of them up in his arms like they were little dolls. When he stood, they'd all gather around him—and come up to his knee. He truly was a gentle giant.

The next year, 1982, is when Vince Jr. started to turn wrestling into major American entertainment. Up until then, World Wrestling Entertainment was doing well, but it was still small and operated pretty much only in the Northeast. It was still set up the old way, with different promoters who all had separate territories. Well, Vince Jr. bought out Daddy Vince and set about turning World Wrestling Entertainment into an empire.

"When I was a kid," I remember Vince Jr. saying back then, "my philosophy was, if I wanted something and somebody else didn't want me to have it, the worst that could happen was I might get the hell kicked out of me. So we're going to disassociate ourselves from the other promoters and make a lot of enemies all at once."

And it was a stroke of genius. Vince even admitted that his dad might not have approved of his plans. "Had my dad known at the time I bought him out what my plans were," he said, "he would never have sold his stock to me."

I'm not sure. Daddy Vince was pretty shrewd, and he must have seen the changes that were coming. Vince Jr. certainly saw that videotape and cable TV meant that he could take his shows to a national audience.

But there's no question that beginning in 1982, Vince Jr. turned off a lot of the old-school wrestling people. They got on him because, they'd say, his shows were taking a turn for the ridiculous. Wrestling had always been entertainment, but a lot of people didn't like how far Vince took that.

Well, if you ask me, a lot of the bellyaching was just sour grapes. Like I said before, wrestling has always been entertainment. Vince just made it more entertaining. The scripts and story lines he came up with didn't mean that when we wrestled, we weren't still doing the moves. I defy anyone to look at tapes of my matches and say they're not watching an athlete at work.

You knew that wrestling and entertainment were becoming one and the same when, in the early eighties, a real pain-in-the-ass Hollywood comedian started making news by being a wrestler. His name was Andy Kaufman, and he was a star on the sitcom *Taxi*. All of a sudden he named himself the World InterGender Wrestling Champion, and he challenged women in the ring—even offering one thousand dollars to any woman who could pin him. He and Jerry Lawler got into a feud that ended up on national TV, right there on *Late Night with David Letterman*, when Kaufman threw Letterman's

coffee in Lawler's face. Around this time, Kaufman was trying to get me or some of my girls to wrestle him. I'd tell my girls, "Don't you dare lower yourself so much as to wrestle that idiot!"

One night he came to my dressing room in Madison Square Garden, trying to get me to wrestle him. I just got up from my chair and grabbed him by the seat of his pants and by the scruff of his scrawny neck and tossed him out the door like yesterday's garbage—and kicked his ass for good measure once he landed. Just then Daddy Vince came walking down the hallway and saw what I was up to. I don't believe I'd ever heard Daddy Vince laugh quite so hard as when I manhandled that little shit.

But by then it was Vince Jr. who was running things, and he had a knack for making the story lines connect to what was going on in the world—and the fans loved that. In the early 1980s, for instance, we were all still getting over having our people taken hostage in Iran. Well, what does Vince do but come up with the villain of villains, the Iron Sheik. Born in Tehran, he was a member of the Iranian Olympic Greco-Roman team in 1968, and he claimed he was once the shah's bodyguard. He'd wear *Arabian Nights* wrestling boots with curled toes, and when he'd stomp his boots against the mat, a secret spring would release iron spikes shooting out through the toes—so a kick would become a gouge. His favorite move was the Camel Clutch, which he'd say drew all the blood out of its victim's brain. At a time when everybody was madder than hell at the country of Iran, the Iron Sheik was a brilliant character.

In my humble opinion, the Iron Sheik's match against Hulk Hogan in 1984 did a lot to make wrestling take off the way it did. It was classic good vs. evil stuff. Hulk was the good guy, an all-American golden boy. Actually, a lot of us had known Hulk for a while. He used to come to our shows in Tampa, where he was playing in a rock band, and he got his start by coming up to us wrestlers outside the arena and saying "Can I take your bags in?" That's how he'd get in for free. He always wanted to wrestle. He got his start as a second-tier bad guy named Sterling Golden. But then he played a bad guy named Thunderlips in *Rocky III*, and the Hulkster was born. Pretty soon, Hulkamania would sweep the country, and everywhere you turned, you'd see magazines with his face on the cover, and pretty soon Hulk action figures were everywhere.

It all started with that championship match in 1984 against the Sheik, who had just defeated Bob Backlund for the championship. Hogan replaced the injured Backlund for the rematch. The Iron Sheik tried to get Hogan into one of his dreaded Camel Clutch submission holds, but Hogan reversed out of it and pinned him.

That match had a lot to do with why wrestling was becoming so popular. And, boy, was it ever popular. By 1985, 25 million people made up our weekly TV audience, and four of the top ten cable TV shows were televised wrestling matches. I think some of those

people loved to watch us because all the other sports were getting so damned boring. In football, they were outlawing the endzone spike and sack dances and they seemed to call a penalty on every play. In wrestling, at least, the fans knew they'd be seeing some down and dirty brawling, where it was okay to kick an opponent when she's down. Expected, even.

Plus, how much can your average sports fan really relate to some of these million-dollar prima donnas who play sports nowadays? We had a bond with the fans, even if that involved sometimes jumping into a group of them and kicking their behinds. I loved the fans, but some wrestlers used to make fun of them. One joke that was going around went like this: "What has fourteen teeth and an IQ of fifty?" The answer: "The first ten rows of any wrestling crowd." Now, that's funny, but I've got to say that even the wrestlers who said those kinds of things were just teasing our fans out of love. We knew that we had the most loyal fans in the world, and you could tell we knew that by how much we played to them. Unlike so many of the so-called real athletes, we never pretended we weren't out there putting on a show for you, the paying customer.

Now, I guess I have to toot my own horn here a little and say that I had something to do with the way wrestling was becoming popular, too. Though most of the credit should go to Vince. I know it's hard to believe, but I was getting older in the early eighties—my fifth decade of wrestling professionally. It was clear I was going to have to start grooming a girl who could come along and whip me. It was clear that would have to be the Texas Cowgirl.

That was Wendi Richter, who showed up on my doorstep straight from Dallas, Texas, and said she wanted to be a wrestler. She was tall, lean, and pretty, and I taught her the moves. She always was a bit clumsy, though. I remember one night when she fell into the ring while standing just outside the ropes. "I've heard of people falling out of the ring," I told her, "but never into it."

But the fans seemed to like her, mostly because she had a real heavy Texas drawl. She didn't talk too well, but that awkwardness in interviews made her more likable, I guess. But what really made her popular was something she had no control over. It was the result of another brilliant brainstorm by Vince: the "Rock 'n' Wrestlin' Connection."

Wrestling in the early to mid-eighties was already wildly popular, but the connection between rock music and World Wrestling Entertainment catapulted us to heights we never dreamed of. It started on a plane ride to Puerto Rico; Captain Lou Albano was on the flight. Now, big, fat, hairy Captain Lou is a legendary manager who was once a successful tag-team wrestler. In 1967, he and Tony Altimore won the World Wrestling Entertainment Tag-Team Championships. He went on to manage more than ten World Tag-Team Champions, including the Moondogs and Headshrinkers. As a

manager, he sure was colorful. He used to say he trained his wrestlers on a diet of unborn goat's milk. Anyway, Captain Lou got to talking on this plane with a young girl who was a big-time wrestling fan. Her name was Cyndi Lauper.

Cyndi was already a recording star, but not quite a household name yet. She hit it off with Captain Lou and asked him to be in her upcoming video for the song "Girls Just Want to Have Fun." He played her father in the video and the song went on to be a number one hit. In fact, her debut album, *She's So Unusual*, would go on to produce four top-five hits.

Well, when Captain Lou started telling Vince about how much of a fan Cyndi Lauper was, a lightbulb went on over Vince's head. That man is always thinking. He booked Cyndi, along with Captain Lou, on Rowdy Roddy Piper's interview show, *Piper's Pit*.

As soon as I heard about this show, I knew I didn't want to miss it. Anytime you get three wacky personalities on one show, you know sparks are going to fly. Roddy might have been the strangest of the three. He was the heel of all heels, but he was always a fan favorite. He claimed to come from Scotland—they called him "The Bad Plaid"—and he always wore a skirt into the ring, where he'd often use brass knuckles to lay out his opponents. His interview show went over the edge, too. Once, he tried to make Jimmy "Superfly" Snuka, who came from the Fiji Islands, feel at home, so he gave him a bag of tropical fruit. When Jimmy didn't thank Roddy

quick enough, Roddy hit him over the head with a coconut and rubbed a banana in his face.

As you might imagine, it sure was a riot when Cyndi went on *Piper's Pit*, a show where anything would go. (Vince Jr. hosted a show around this same time, *Tuesday Night Titans*, that was just as outrageous. Guest wrestlers would chat with Vince, belt each other, and eat the furniture; once, the wrestler Kamala ate live chickens during an interview!) On Roddy's show, Albano tried to take credit for Cyndi's success and then called her a "broad." Well, that little rock-and-roller started clobbering both Albano and Piper over the head with her purse, calling Captain Lou a "fat bag of wind" and "an amoeba." "Tell you what, fat man—I'm going to put a woman up against one of your choice," she said. "And if my woman wins, you're going to have to apologize and admit that women are as good as men!"

The next day, my phone rang. It was Captain Lou.

"Hey, you fat bag of wind!" I yelled.

"Is that the amoeba?" Mae called from the kitchen, laughing.

"Yeah," I said, wanting to tease the fat bastard even more. "He's calling 'cause he got beat up by a little rock-and-roller and he needs our help!"

We were sure having a good laugh at his expense. Of course, that was why he was calling. He didn't know who Cyndi was about to choose to represent her in the ring, but he knew that being with Moolah was smarter than being against her.

Well, Cyndi asked Wendi Richter to wrestle for her, and it was a smart choice. That set up my championship fight on July 23, 1984, against Wendi at Madison Square Garden—broadcast live, of all places, on MTV, thanks to Cyndi's involvement. Cyndi and Wendi came into the ring while the PA system blared "Girls Just Want to Have Fun," and the crowd went crazy. A lot of new fans were coming to wrestling because of Cyndi. I remember looking out at the crowd that night and seeing groups of young teenage girls, dressed just like Cyndi and with that crazy bright red hair, holding "Girls Just Want to Have Fun" signs.

I love those high-pressure matches, and I started out strong. Wendi had long hair, just like I like it, and I tossed her out of the ring by a handful of it while the crowd oohed and ahhed. I roughed her up pretty good on the hard concrete outside the ring while the crowd got all revved up. Once we got back inside the squared circle, though, things started going against me. Wendi started going on the offensive when I got caught against the ropes and found myself sneak-attacked by Cyndi. She came up behind me and, from outside the ropes, started pounding me over the head with her pocketbook—the same one she'd used against Roddy and Captain Lou on TV. That thing gave me some welts, because she weighed it down. She called it her Loaded Purse of Doom, and it did get my head all cloudy. I should have known I was going to be in trouble when, as

Cyndi was sneak-attacking me, I looked at the ref, who was looking right at what was going on and not doing a damn thing.

"Aren't you going to stop her?" I yelled while Cyndi wailed on me from behind and Wendi kicked me in the stomach from the front.

"C'mon, let's wrestle!" the ref said, never making a move to step in.

I guess after all those years of getting away with underhanded acts in the ring, I was getting my due on that night. The law of averages was finally catching up to me. Actually, when I think back on it, I'm sure I'm still way ahead—if you total it up, I've done a lot more damage in sneaky ways than I had done to me.

But that night against Wendi, I sure did feel like I was robbed. We went back and forth, each of us turning the tables on the other. Finally, at the end, we got ourselves into a pin combination, where I had her shoulders against the mat and she had mine the same way. You don't find yourself in that kind of situation too often. That no-good bastard ref started counting, and it became a question of who could get their shoulder off the mat first, me or Wendi. Well, to this day, I know damn well I got my left shoulder up before her, and when he called the match right there I was about to start celebrating. But then I saw Wendi jump up all happy like, and Cyndi came running into the ring, celebrating, and I knew I'd been had. I made a beeline for that short ref and started beating the tar out of

him while Wendi and Cyndi were jumping around and the tune "Girls Just Want to Have Fun" came on over the loudspeaker. They brought that championship belt—*my championship belt!*—into the ring, and there were these two fools, holding up what had been around my waist for twenty-eight years! They were prancing around the ring, acting as if what belonged to me was now theirs, and I just

Lillian Ellison

took out all my frustration on that poor ref, who was a quivering, bruised mess by the time Captain Lou dragged me away from him.

I was heartbroken for a while at losing my championship. Of course, I knew everybody was right when they said I had had an amazing run, that twenty-eight years of being a champion is unheard of, but it still hurt. I guess that's because, unlike a lot of the girls who were coming into wrestling, I never looked at wrestling as a stepping-stone to anything else. A lot of them—especially since the Rock 'n' Wrestlin' Connection—looked at getting in the ring like it was a way to become a star. Me, I never thought about it like that. I always was a competitor and I always wanted just to kick butt in the squared circle.

By the way, that's what did Wendi in, I think. She got all caught up in being a celebrity and forgot that being a wrestler is what she was. For example, Cyndi had a bunch of us wrestlers appear in her videos, and Wendi just loved it. Me? I hated it. Because it wasn't what I do.

They flew me out to California to shoot Cyndi's "Goonies 'R' Good Enough" video. Now, Captain Lou had already played Cyndi's father in the "Girls Just Want to Have Fun" video, and he also appeared in her "Time After Time" and "She Bop" videos. Wendi was the waitress blowing a bubble and singing the first verse in the "She Bop" video.

I joined a bunch of other wrestlers for the "Goonies" video. Rowdy Roddy, the Iron Sheik, and I played the band of pirates who chased Cyndi underground. Playing the Goonie kids were a group of Hollywood child actors who would later go on to become stars themselves. There was Sean Astin, Corey Feldman, Josh Brolin, and Martha Plimpton.

"The wrestlers were a pain in the ass," Cyndi later told the press. "The *Goonie* kids loved the wrestlers, but the Iron Sheik was so rotten; he made the kids cry because they were being a little rowdy. He yelled at them and gave them a scare."

She was right about the Iron Sheik—he was a piece of work, and he'd be a pain to anyone he came into contact with, adult or child. But maybe I was guilty of being a pain in the ass, too, because I was miserable. I found that whole video experience to be horrible, just horrible. I realized then and there that I don't ever want to do any movie or stuff like that. Leave that to the likes of Wendi, Hulk, and The Rock. I'm a wrestler, and I'd rather go and wrestle a six-out-of-ten-falls match night after night than go through that stuff.

It was just so aggravating. You've got to get up at four in the morning because they send a limousine for you at five to take you to the studio. There, they have what they call breakfast. Yeah, right. Stale coffee and a Danish, if you're lucky. Then they take you to the makeup room, where they spend all this time doing you up just so, so you can sit some more and wait. They tell you you're due to go on at noon, but then lunchtime comes, so you've got to eat some crusty sandwich that tastes like cardboard. Then they retouch your

Lillian Ellison

makeup, because you've been sweating. And then you wait some more. After "dinner," they tell you, "We've got to wait till later on tonight." By eleven, it's gotten too late, and they tell you the shoot will be the first thing they do the next morning.

It's funny how people think being in videos, movies, or on TV is all glamorous. Let me tell you, it's not all it's cracked up to be. I'd just as soon never have to put up with another video or photo shoot. I guess some people like that kind of hassle, but it's not for me. Being the champ seemed to go right to Wendi's head, and she loved all that "star" crap. Like I said, that's not who I am.

After losing my championship, I started concentrating really hard on making history by winning it back. This was in 1985, and I was very mindful of the example set by Muhammad Ali back in the seventies when he came back to win the boxing title for a record third time. If he could make history, why couldn't I?

But I knew it wouldn't be easy. Thanks to her relationship with Cyndi, Wendi was a crowd favorite. I was used to having the fans go against me, but Wendi was so popular now, I couldn't count on the refs to do their jobs. I realized that the first step on my comeback trail involved flat out stopping Wendi. She was running around the country and ducking giving me a rematch, so I started focusing on the next best thing—managing a challenger who had a shot against her. One way or another, revenge would be mine.

On February 18, 1985, I managed Leilani Kai in a championship bout against Wendi at Madison Square Garden. Leilani had lots of talent, and she had me on her side. That night I circled the ring, looking for my opportunity to jump into the rumble and give Wendi a shot or two. Cyndi was there, too, screaming through the whole match in that high, squeaky voice of hers.

I sure did teach Leilani well. I had her grabbing clumps of Wendi's hair and throwing her all around the ring. Once, Leilani had Wendi in a tight chokehold right by the ropes, where I was standing. Cyndi came over there, too, as I yelled out, "Break her neck, Leilani!"

The match was a tough battle, and when Wendi slammed Leilani to the mat, it looked like it was about to be over. As Leilani lay motionless on the ground, Wendi was about to cover her. There was no doubt it would be a three-count, and that would be it. I knew I'd have to do something quick. I ran over to where Cyndi was outside the ring and, grabbing her, got two hands around her neck. The crowd started roaring, and Cyndi's face turned blue and her eyes took on this faraway look. Her boyfriend and manager Dave Wolff came charging over from the crowd, trying to pull Cyndi away from me. In the ring, Wendi must have heard the crowd, and she looked over just as she was about to pounce on Leilani. Wendi came running over to get me off her manager, and I pretended like I didn't see her. Just as she bent over the ropes for me, I hauled back and—

pow!—socked her right in the throat. She staggered back, her knees buckled, and she went down. Leilani got to her feet and jumped on the champ, while Cyndi, right next to me, slumped to the concrete, unconscious. Suddenly the ref counted to three and the bell rang. I jumped into the ring, and there lay Wendi on the mat, so I kicked her for good measure.

Leilani and I started jumping up and down when the ref handed us the championship belt. Cyndi and Wendi came running into the ring after us and we took off—me and the new champ. Boy, were Cyndi and Wendi pissed.

Wouldn't you know Wendi started bellyaching for a rematch, even though she hadn't given me one. I had to resort to managing someone else to whip her. Truth be told, though, I sure felt that Leilani's victory was my victory, because she would never have done it without everything I'd taught her. Besides, she might not have won it if it wasn't for my shot to Wendi's throat that laid her flat out on the canvas.

Vince was planning the biggest of promotions at the Garden for late the following month. It would be called *WrestleMania* and one of the featured matches would be the rematch between Leilani and Wendi. Little did we know it then, but *WrestleMania* would change the face of wrestling. It would be Vince's legacy. And to this day I'm proud to have been a part of it.

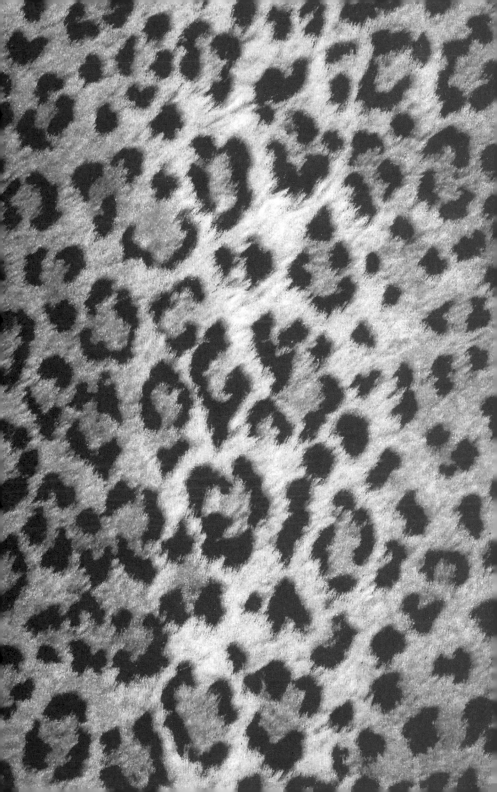

11

"So Long, Champ!"

THERE YOU GO THINKING AGAIN!"

That's what I used to say to Vince in those days, when he pretty much single-handedly put wrestling over the top and made it into blockbuster American entertainment.

See, Vince learned from the buzz of the Andy Kaufman/Jerry Lawler feud and the Rock 'n' Wrestlin' Connection. He knew to think big, and the bigger he thought, the bigger the payoff would be. That's how he came up with *WrestleMania*. Now that there have been so many of them, it's easy to forget just how wild an idea it was in 1985.

Vince knew that World Wrestling Entertainment was in the entertainment business, and that we were no different from Hollywood and Broadway. So he borrowed from those entertainment examples and started planning blockbusters, bringing in celebrities to make the events hip. He looked at how many Americans watched

Lillian Ellison

the Super Bowl and decided to come up with a Super Bowl for wrestling. There would be only one big difference. The Super Bowl was usually a crappy game, where the players play real scared and one team runs up the score on the other. *WrestleMania*, however, would provide more action and excitement than anything ever before.

So on March 31, 1985, *WrestleMania* dawned. It was sold out at Madison Square Garden, and it was beamed live to two hundred closed-circuit outlets throughout the country. Ringside tickets cost $100, and *WrestleMania* T-shirts were $14.75. The hype leading up to that night was unheard of, even by wrestling's standards. The main event was Hulk Hogan and Mr. T against Roddy Piper and "Mr. Wonderful" Paul Orndorff. Hulk and Mr. T were going to be defending the honor of none other than Cyndi Lauper, who "Rowdy" Roddy had been attacking. Days before the match, Hulk—everybody's favorite wrestler—seemed to be on every TV station at the same time, giving interview after interview. On one show, a comedian by the name of Richard Belzer asked the Hulkster to demonstrate a wrestling hold. Well, Hulk put him in a front chinlock, and wouldn't you know that comic's eyes rolled back into his head and he slumped to the ground unconscious. He woke up moments later, and his head was bleeding all over the place. He needed eight stitches and whined like a little baby about what Hulk had done to him, but not before taking out a full-page ad in the *New York Post* to announce that the incident would be replayed five nights later!

MTV got into the act, too. On the air, the station kept showing interviews with feminist leader Gloria Steinem and recent vice-presidential nominee Geraldine Ferraro that made it look like both women were attending wrestling matches. In reality, both were at Steinem's *Ms.* magazine's Women of the Year breakfast some months before, as was Cyndi. It was there that she asked each to say something about Piper, and they went along with the joke. "He's not fit to wear a skirt," said Steinem. Ferraro challenged Piper to "Come out and fight like a man."

Well, MTV started showing these clips over and over again, and both women complained that it made them seem like they were endorsing World Wrestling Entertainment. Ferraro whined that she had been assured her comments would be used in "good taste." Now, I just had to laugh at that. Here's this woman who, when she wanted to be vice-president, told us all to trust her judgment about things—and she was admitting that she thought World Wrestling Entertainment would do something in good taste? Right then, I knew she wasn't fit to be in public office.

There was always electricity in the air for wrestling at the Garden, but when the big night came, it was even more thrilling than ever before. Backstage, everywhere you turned, you saw a celebrity. There was the Yankees then-manager Billy Martin, the night's ring announcer. Liberace, who would be the guest timekeeper, pranced

around. For maybe the first time in his life, he wasn't the most wildly dressed man in the room. Dressed in his pink, tie-dyed tuxedo, Jesse "The Body" Ventura looked nothing like a future governor. Long-time manager Classy Freddie Blassie was dressed in a sparkling red costume that gave you a headache if you looked directly at it for too long. Muhammad Ali was the guest referee, and this was before he lost most of his ability to speak due to Parkinson's disease. I never thought I'd be in a room where Ali was barely noticeable because of all the loud characters buzzing around nearby.

Roddy Piper walked around with his sixteen-member bagpipe band, and when that crazy Iron Sheik came in, he called out, "Where is that stupid woman Cyndi Lauper?" Everyone laughed when you heard Cyndi's tiny voice yell back to the bald Sheik, "Where's the hair on your head?"

As far as the matches go, the one that would always be re-membered would be the main event. Hulk Hogan was having a tough time of it. He was kneed, whacked across the back with a folding chair, and gouged senseless. At one point he couldn't reach the outstretched hand of his partner, Mr. T, and it looked like the good guys were about to go down. That's what I wanted, of course—since I always root for the bad guys.

Anyway, Mr. Wonderful got Hulk in a full nelson and "Ace" Orton, who had been in Roddy and Mr. Wonderful's corner with his arm in a plastic cast, came charging into the ring. He wound up and was about to cream the Hulkster with his club of a cast—only he missed and hit Mr. Wonderful instead. Mr. Wonderful fell to the mat, unconscious, and Hulk covered him for the pin while the Garden crowd roared.

It was such an exciting finish that hardly anyone remembered the outcome of the rematch between Wendi Richter and Leilani Kai. Wendi won back her championship, mainly because Cyndi kept me from getting too involved in the match. She kept coming after me outside the ring, and that meant I couldn't distract Wendi like I'd done the month before, when I enabled Leilani to get the surprise pin on Wendi and win the championship.

Well, there was no such luck at *WrestleMania*. Wendi won and she and Cyndi started dancing around that ring. By now, I was damned sick of that "Girls Just Want to Have Fun" song. After the match, people asked me about Cyndi. "If they just left me alone with her for a few seconds more," I said, "I'd have had her to the point where she wouldn't be singing anymore."

So Wendi was the champ again. Now, you ought to know by now that I don't ever go out of my way to say an unkind word about anyone, especially anyone who shares my profession. But I don't mind telling you that around about this time I stopped liking Wendi Richter.

This is the way it was. At first, I was trying to help Wendi every way I could. She came to me a youngster fresh from Dallas, and I tried to

see to it that I did right by her. But remember how I've told you that a lot of people, when they make it big, change? They forget where they came from? Just the way I'd seen Mildred Burke seem to stop having time for people who were just like she had been, I started to see how Wendi was going through a Jekyll and Hyde transformation.

In the beginning, Wendi had seemed to want to be a wrestler, not just be in the limelight. But once she got that championship, that's when her behavior started to change.

One night we were in Canada, and we had to drive from Vancouver to Calgary. The Russian Nikolai Volkoff was driving. He was a 325-pounder with a chest that measured sixty-five inches. He had recently destroyed the 400-pound Gorilla Monsoon in all of four minutes. While he'd never won the championship, he was the tag-team champ, along with his partner, that crazy Iron Sheik, who was also along for the ride.

Wendi was in the backseat with the Iron Sheik, and Nikolai and I were in the front. Nikolai was a nice man, and he didn't drink or smoke, just like me. Pretty soon I smelled smoke and my eyes started watering and I started coughing. Well, Wendi and the Iron Sheik started giggling in the backseat, where they had lit up cigarettes. They thought it was a real joke, while I'm sitting there, getting sick from the smell.

"I'm gonna tell you, it takes a low-down dirty bastard to pull tricks like this," I yelled at them. "If you have to smoke, why don't you do it when you get to your hotel room? Respect other people if you can't respect yourself!"

The Iron Sheik started cussing back, and Wendi was laughing but they kept right on. It was wintertime, but we had to open the windows because of the smoke. When we got to Calgary, I found the promoter Stu Hart. Stu was the father of Bret and Owen Hart.

"If you don't mind," I said, "I'd like you to get me a commercial flight back to New York."

"Why, Moolah?"

"Because I want to sleep tonight," I said, going on to tell him what I had just gone through.

"Moolah," he said, "you ought to just beat the hell out of her and take the championship back."

"That's not even the thing," I said. "I just want to get away from it all."

So I did my show and then flew back to the States and called Vince. I told him I was sick for two or three days from being exposed to the smoke. Well, Vince hit the roof. He got Wendi on the phone and told her, "You're gonna have to straighten up."

"I wasn't smoking," she said, in that Texas accent of hers.

"Well, I don't think Moolah would lie about it," Vince said.

"I don't care what Lil says," Wendi said.

I used to warn the girls all the time that a lot of times, the male Superstars would say things to them just to start trouble. Some-

times, when the women were doing well, the men would say things because they were jealous. One day the Iron Sheik said to Wendi, "You were supposed to get fifty thousand dollars for *WrestleMania*. That's what I got."

So Wendi came complaining to me. "We got cheated out of our money," she says.

"What do you mean?" I asked.

"We were supposed to get fifty thousand dollars," she said.

"Bullshit," I said. "Vince McMahon is not that kind of man. What you were supposed to get, you got."

"Well, I'm gonna tell him I want my money, and I want it now!"

"You better keep your mouth shut," I told her. "You're forgetting that you were serving Wendy's hamburgers out of a drive-through window for three bucks an hour before Vince McMahon. You better be damned happy and keep your mouth shut. And you better believe it was an honest payoff if Vince McMahon gave it to you!"

Well, that girl didn't take my advice. She stormed in on Vince and told him she wanted the rest of her money. He looked at her like she was crazy, and then she demanded *her* fifty thousand. Now, I told you that Vince is the sweetest man I've ever met, but not if you cross him. He kicked her out of his office, and I told Wendi after that: "I think you made a helluva mistake by doing what I told you not to do."

Then she started talking about how she was going to retire with the championship, just like June Byers tried to do years before. Well, it didn't work then, and it wouldn't work in the eighties, either. Pretty soon, Vince called me. I had been managing Penny Mitchell as the Spider Lady. She'd get dressed up in this black-widow costume with a spider mask on her face and a lot of people had fun trying to guess who that was in disguise. Well, Vince sug-

gested that I wear the Spider Lady outfit for a shot at Wendi—that very night. "I want to see who is the toughest, once and for all," he said, and he told me not to say a word to anyone.

I was by my nephew's bedside in the Columbia hospital, where he had been diagnosed with cancer. I hopped in one of my Caddies and sped across the highways. Between driving and being so upset about my nephew, I didn't sleep for about four nights when, on November 25, 1985, the championship was up for grabs between Wendi and the Spider Lady (me).

Boy, was this ever a classic match. Jesse "The Body" Ventura and Gorilla Monsoon were ringside, announcing the match for TV. Early on, I—er, I'm sorry, the Spider Lady—got Wendi on the ropes and put her in a tight choke hold before kicking her out onto the concrete. "Maybe that's Moolah!" Jesse commented, and everybody thought it was just a joke, because up till now, I'd always been side by side with the Spider Lady, managing her. But that was when it was Penny inside that hot-as-heck getup, not me.

Anyway, I was ramming Wendi into the top turnbuckle and then used the top rope around her neck to choke her, right in front of the ref. "This ref is very tentative," Jesse said.

After about eight minutes, I was clotheslined by Wendi, and we both went down. We both got up and came toward each other in the center of the ring. We were both wobbly, but standing face-to-face with her, I managed to get my arms around her neck and roll

her down and over onto her back—in a small package, so her shoulders were against the mat.

"Small package! Nicely executed!" yelled Gorilla Monsoon.

The ref got down and started his count, but it was rushed. Almost exactly at the time he counted three, Wendi kicked up and out of the hold.

"Boy, was that close!" said Monsoon.

Then all heck broke loose. Suddenly the bell sounded.

"What was that?" wondered Monsoon.

"Did the ref make a three-count?" Jesse asked.

Wendi kept at me, but I knew I heard the bell, so I kept putting my hands into the air, to signal that I'd won. I looked out at the stunned crowd—they still didn't know if it was a pin or not—while Wendi got me from behind and tore off my mask.

"It is Moolah!" screamed Monsoon. "Look at that!"

I started running away from Wendi while the crowd was going nuts. She grabbed my hair, and from ringside, Jesse yelled: "We've got chaos in the ring! This is chaos!"

Just then the ref handed me the championship belt, and I hoisted it in the air while Wendi kept trying to toss me here and there by my hair. Ring announcer Howard Finkel came in and grabbed the microphone. "Ladies and gentlemen," he bellowed. "The winner of this contest and the new World Wrestling Entertainment Women's Champion . . ."

Now the place was going wild, once they heard Howard say the word *new*, and Wendi was still taking swings at me and crying at the same time.

". . . the Spider . . ." Howard said, kind of like a question, because he couldn't believe it. "The Fabulous Moolah!"

I clutched at that championship belt, because let me tell you, it had missed its mama. I fought through the crowd and made it back to the dressing room, where I just stood, waiting for Wendi, because I knew I was going to have to do it all over again back there, away from the crowd and the cameras. I couldn't celebrate or think about what the moment meant, since I figured she and I had some unfinished business.

Well, she came charging in and didn't even look at me. She just up and grabbed her suitcase and didn't even change. She stormed out of Madison Square Garden with her tights still on. I just smiled, waved, and called after her, "So long, champ!"

That's the last I saw of Wendi Richter. I hear she's somewhere in Florida now, selling real estate. I got in my car and hightailed it back to Columbia, where I could be with my nephew. During the long drive, it all started to sink in. I found a good country-music station and some old songs of my old sweetheart Hank Williams came on, and I thought about how I started out as a little girl wanting to be a champion, and here I was, still winning championships. And I thought about everyone who helped me along the way and how proud they'd be—from Hank to Buddy to my mama and daddy, and from my brothers to Jack Pfeffer to sweet old Elvis. I try not to look back too often, because there ain't much point in dwelling on what's already happened. But that night, on a clear road with Hank and Conway and Johnny Cash ringing in my ears, I thought back and felt like the luckiest girl on earth. By the time I got into Columbia, I was done covering old ground. I looked into that rearview mirror and said to the butt kicker I saw there, "You ain't even done yet."

Lillian Ellison

12

THE SIXTH DECADE

A LOT OF TIMES MAE, KATIE, AND I like to sit around and watch sports on the boob tube. And maybe you do this, too: We find ourselves laughing at the dumb things the announcers say, those blow-dried blowhards who, many times, ain't never done what it is they're announcing about. We just shake our heads as the clichés fly.

But it's a funny thing about clichés; they come into being because they were once true. And they've kept an element of truth to them over the years, even if they're overused and misunderstood. Well, beginning in 1986, I think I ran smack-dab into the truth of one of those sports clichés.

Let's call it the "fire in the belly" cliché. You know the one: The camera pans in real close on a champion, and the announcer talks about how the champ's dominance comes from wanting it more than the next guy, from having that extra bit of desire, that "fire in

Lillian Ellison

the belly" to excel. I think that's pretty much true. Skill doesn't separate those at the top level of a field as much as attitude.

Well, for twenty-eight years, I had the attitude of a champion. I walked into an arena, and I exuded confidence. I was not going to be beat. But even after winning my championship back as the Spider Lady, I had a different kind of feeling. It was more like, well, you lost once, you can lose again. And if I was feeling this way—just a tad less confident—then surely the other girls were looking at me differently, too, maybe sensing a little bit of vulnerability there for the first time.

I think that's what explains what happened in 1986 and then in 1987. In July 1986, I went down under to Australia to defend my championship a whole lot of nights in a row. I sure did like Australia; the countryside is beautiful and the people are friendly, even if they do talk funny.

Come to think of it, wrestling has sent me all over the world, and I pretty much have loved everywhere I've visited. Okay, Japan I wasn't too crazy about. I couldn't eat their food and lost about eighteen pounds over there. I'd ask for chicken and they'd bring me some disfigured, fishy-smelling, raw-looking thing. "That ain't chicken!" I'd scream. "Take it away!" I noticed that out on the street, I never did see any dogs or cats, and I was starting to suspect they were trying to feed me house pets.

Anyway, on July 3, 1986, I lost my championship to Velvet McIntyre in Brisbane, Australia. The reason I don't really count this as

a title loss is because, six nights later, I got it right back from her. Technically, it was a title loss, but by the time news of it made its way back to the States, my championship belt was already back around my waist.

I spent the next year winning matches, until squaring off against Sensational Sherri Martel in Houston, Texas, on July 24, 1987. Most people in wrestling hadn't heard of Sherri yet. She was considered a newcomer. But, unfortunately, I was already real familiar with her.

Like so many girls who wanted to break into the business, she showed up on my doorstep, looking to be taught. I took her in, rented her an apartment on my property. But she turned out to be one of those girls who had a problem living by my rules. She liked nightclubbing and going out, and that just didn't go with me.

So I showed her the highway, because she wasn't about to do things my way. She had some talent, though, and as the years passed she developed a sense of ring showmanship. For instance, a lot of the men, like Sting and the Ultimate Warrior, took to wearing face paint in the ring. Sherri was one of the first women to do the same, using different designs to reflect her moods. She'd wear a silver painted-on tear or a heart—anything to add a sense of style to her character.

She wasn't wearing any paint that night in Houston, though. I came out and started putting a good old-fashioned whupping on her. It must have been six or seven times that I knocked her out of

the ring and onto the concrete floor. Since I was so in control, I don't know if I just got careless or cocky or what. But one of those times when she was sprawled out on the concrete, I lifted her to her feet by her hair and brought her over to the ring and started to suplex her back over the ropes; once back in the ring, I sure as heck was going to cover her for the pin.

It didn't quite work out like that. Everything happened so quickly; somehow, just as I got her on the mat and went for the cover, she reversed out of it and put me down. I was stunned, because everything up until that point had been going my way. The next thing I knew, *she* was covering *me*, and the ref slammed the mat three times. I was just lying there, flat on my back, not hurt, but shocked. Just like that, the championship was taken from me.

To call that loss an upset would be an understatement. It had a real impact—and not just on me. You know, I don't like to sound like I'm bragging or giving myself more credit than I deserve. But a lot of people tell me that they trace the decline of women's wrestling to what happened that night. Just two years before that, Wendi and I were wrestling on MTV, starring in videos, having articles written about us, and playing to packed houses. After Sherri won the championship, though, there was no more interest in women's wrestling. The next October, Sherri lost the championship to Rockin' Robin in Paris; not long after that, the championship was vacated and abandoned because of inactivity. No women were wrestling any-more, and the few who wanted to couldn't draw an audience.

Sherri came back on the scene in the early nineties, but not as a wrestler; this time she was a valet to "Macho Man" Randy Savage, after he turned heel. As the nineties went on, women's wrestling came back, but not so much for the wrestling. The moves took a backseat to things like whether or not the loser would end up in her underwear. I'm sure Daddy Vince was gyrating in his grave when the first "Evening Gown" match took place—two girls facing off dressed in evening gowns instead of wrestling tights, and the first to rip the gown off the other was the winner. I was a bit taken aback at first, too. But I also had to admit that some of those shows were funny as all get out, and they sure kept me and Mae and Katie entertained.

I don't know whether I got out of wrestling at the right time, or if women's wrestling hit the doldrums because I got out of wrestling. That's for others to decide, I reckon. What I know is that beginning in the early nineties—my sixth decade inside the squared circle—the road was no longer my real home. I still traveled around once in a while and put on some exhibitions, but it wasn't like it used to be. Mostly, I stayed in Columbia and continued to train girls.

Around this time, Verne Langdon asked me to come to Los An-geles and help him open a wrestling gym called Slammers. I first met Verne when I went to Hollywood to do the videos with Cyndi Lauper. He was my makeup man, and we struck up a great friend-

ship. He once invited me to his house, where I met a lot of the stars of the daytime soap operas. He loved wrestling and wanted to be a part of it, so I jumped at the chance to help him with his school.

When I was teaching wrestling there, it was funny how surprised they'd get when it dawned on them that there really is a lot to know if you're going to wrestle and be any good at it. For example, a lot of people don't know that the wrestling ring is smaller than a boxing ring and that there are three ropes around the side of the ring instead of the four used in boxing. I'd spend whole days just teaching rope work, because being able to use the ropes to your advantage is key to being a wrestler. You've got to know how to bounce off the ropes without going through them, and it's easier said than done.

In 1995, I was the first woman ever inducted into the World Wrestling Entertainment Hall of Fame. Vince made me cry when he got up and talked about how all of the good fortune that was happening to wrestling in the nineties wouldn't have been possible if it hadn't been for me. When I spoke, I tried to send that credit right back at the McMahon family, particularly Daddy Vince, who I knew was in that room in spirit.

The other thing I really concentrated on as we got into the mid-nineties was making the Ladies' International Wrestling Association (LIWA) something special. Each year, we gathered in Las Vegas to honor different wrestlers from the past. That's what we were doing when I tried to get that one wrestler to attend, the one I mentioned who couldn't get Jesus on the phone.

Clara Martensen was a member of the LIWA. She was the champ before Mildred Burke, and before she passed away in November 1988, she requested that six ladies of the LIWA be the pallbearers at her funeral. What a sight that was—six ladies carrying a casket. It was me, Mae Weston, Bette Clarke, Theresa Theis, Maria Barnetti, and of course, Mae Young.

1991 ACHIEVEMENT AWARD
EDITORS' AWARD
AS VOTED BY
THE EDITORS OF
PRO WRESTLING ILLUSTRATED
MAGAZINE

That was a sad occasion, because we all loved Clara and were indebted to her. Without her leading the way, we knew we never would have been as successful as we became. But mostly the LIWA conventions sure have been fun. We tracked down a lot of names from the past, and they showed up. Gladys Gilem was there. Her nickname used to be Kill 'Em, and she rassled in carnival shows fifty and sixty years ago, when women's wrestling shared billing with bearded ladies (sometimes the bearded lady and the wrestler were one and the same) and two-headed goats. Was I surprised to find out that she left wrestling to become a lion trainer and alligator wrestler!

I got a chance to catch up with Belle Starr, Bonnie Watson, and Ella Waldeck. Even June Byers showed up, telling us how she still has double vision—ever since a fan threw a bottle at her in Moose Jaw, Saskatchewan, Canada, that hit her right between the eyes.

Of course I wouldn't be behind these get-togethers if all they were was a chance for some beaten-down wrestlers to get together and tell old war stories. No, we also got ourselves back into the ring and took some bumps. In fact, every year from 1995 to 1999, my dear friend Valerie Boesch was my valet when I got back into that squared circle. Valerie is from Houston, Texas, where she and her husband, Paul, were big promoters. They were good friends of the Bush family—as in former President George Herbert Walker Bush—and I always used to joke with Valerie that she should organize a tag-team match, me and former President Bush against all comers; I just knew we'd kick ass.

I don't go in much for politics, but I'm a big fan of the Bushes—both Bush Sr. and his son, our current president. They sure are better role models than Bill and Hillary Clinton—I've spit on better things than those two. Hillary never did act like a first lady, and Bill was nothing but a womanizer. And unlike John F. Kennedy, Bill wasn't even good at it, judging by some of the trash he got into his bed.

Anyway, those LIWA weekends sure were fun. It wasn't just old-timers who got back in the ring, either. What I did was invite promoters from all over the country, and I also invited girls from all around who wanted to break into wrestling. This way, I figured, the weekend could be a sort of tryout for a lot of the girls.

That's how Chyna first came to the attention of World Wrestling Entertainment. She was a sixteen- or seventeen-year-old Sunday-school type girl at the time, real timid. I put her in a tag team match and she did real well. I found Pat Patterson in the audience. Pat was the blond bomber from San Francisco who, in the late seventies and early eighties, got a reputation as one of the best ring psychologists of all time. Now he works for World Wrestling Entertainment in the talent-relations department. We've been friends for years.

"Pat, this girl has a good future," I told him. "She has a muscled-up body, if y'all are looking for somebody like that."

I wasn't in love with Chyna's style, mind you. It wasn't like the traditional wrestling, like I do. But she was doing her style okay. Plus, I respected her because she always looked neat when she was in the ring. If a person comes in looking all sloppy, it's like they don't care about how they're looked at when they're performing. Me, before going into the ring, I had to know my shoestrings were clean, my boots were polished, my socks were snow white. I wanted people to say to themselves, *Why does she have to be so mean and look so nice?*

Chyna was like that; you could tell she cared. A year after she was in World Wrestling Entertaiment, I decided to give her the LIWA Rookie of the Year award. She couldn't make it to the convention to accept the award, so I sent it to her. It was probably a year later that I ran into her at one of the *WrestleManias*.

"Hi, Chyna, do you remember me?" I said.

"Oh, yeah," she said. "Hi." Then she turned her back and headed straight for the dressing room. *Boy,* I remember thinking, *has she changed!* Not even a thank-you for the award.

But then, about a year later, I got a Christmas card from her in which she wrote: "I don't think I ever thanked you for my award, and I wanted you to know I appreciated it." Well, she didn't have to do that. Let that be a lesson, I told myself; she may have just been having a bad day at that *WrestleMania*, but it's never too late to do the right, kind thing, and her sending me that card was right and kind.

As Chyna got bigger and bigger Pat Patterson and I started joking around about a comeback for little old me. At home, Mae and I were still going strong, training girls in the ring when we weren't

throwing each other out of it in some classic knock-down-drag-out wars between a couple of senior citizens. Little did we know that Pat was seriously talking to people—including Vince—about bringing us back.

One day in 1998 the phone rang. On the other end was Vince. It wasn't unusual for him to call just to see how we were doing. But this time the fella who never stopped thinking had an idea.

"How'd you like to make history?" he said. Before I knew it, Mae and I were on a plane. We were coming back. And I had some unfinished business.

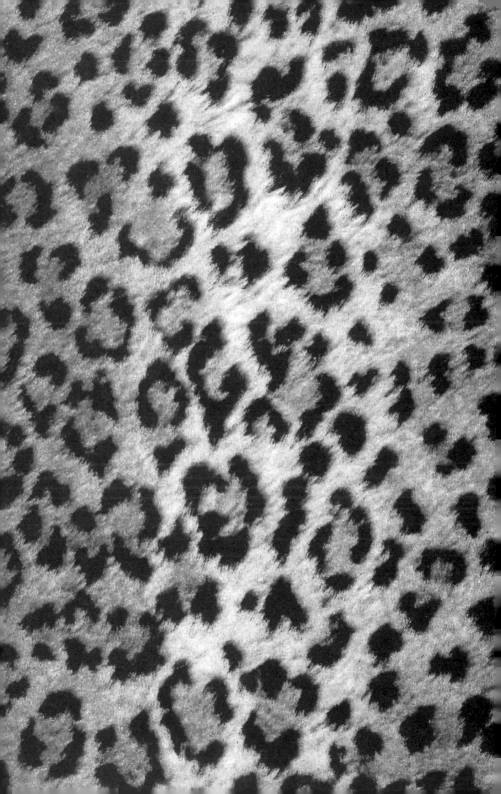

13

THE COMEBACK

WHEN I MADE MY RETURN to World Wrestling Entertainment in 1999, it was like a big family reunion. Even the wrestlers I didn't know knew enough about me that they'd come up and throw their arms around me and give me a greeting like I was a long-lost relative.

In a way, I was. I don't care what decade you do it in, if you've made a living inside that squared circle, performing for people, that bonds you to others who have done the same thing.

For most of my career, it was mostly Daddy Vince running things. But now the family atmosphere was even more obvious, because the whole McMahon family was involved. Vince and his lovely wife, Linda, would be there, along with Stephanie and Shane. They sent me our schedule and plane tickets—no more of that driving-cross-country stuff. And Mae and I ended up doing the Pay-Per-Views, *WrestleMania*, *SmackDown!*, and *Raw*. We were in the wedding show with Stephanie and Triple H, who is one of my favorite young men. His daddy came to a lot of the shows, and Triple H looks just like him. I've always believed you can judge a young fella by how he treats his father, and Triple H—which stands for Hunter Hearst Helmsley—is very respectful to all his elders.

Anyway, Mae and I would get to the arena early on the afternoon of a show. Vince would have put out a big lunch buffet for all the Superstars, World Wrestling Entertainment staff, and TV production people, and we'd chow down while we went over that night's script. It would take a few hours to memorize the story lines and our lines.

One of our first story lines had to do with Jeff Jarrett. He was quite a character. He declared himself the greatest living country-western singer, even though when he burst into song in the ring, it sounded like nails screeching across a chalkboard. His signature finishing move was to bring his guitar crashing down onto the head of his opponent.

The fans loved that move, and Vince and I had quite a chuckle about it, since he knew that I'd remember where it really came from. A while back, the Honky Tonk Man would bring a guitar to the ring with him, because he called himself the second coming of Elvis. Well, like Double J, he was no rival to the real King when it came to carrying a tune. But he found another way to express his musical talents—by smashing his guitar over his opponents' heads.

It just goes to show that a good act is a good act, no matter when it's performed. Anyway, Vince wanted to know if I'd come back in a story line with Jeff Jarrett.

"I'll come back with anybody," I said. "I'm ready to kick ass and take names."

So Jeff Jarrett invited me up to the ring, wanting to show me respect by introducing me to the audience. Around this time Chyna had challenged him to a match, and he asked me right there what did I think of that. "Well," I said, pausing dramatically to get the crowd all riled up. "I've wrestled men before, and I've kicked their butts . . . just like Chyna's going to kick yours!"

The place went wild, and the next thing you know, I'm lying out cold on the mat because Double J had whacked me over the head with the guitar. That's the first time I realized just how much these young fans were going to love old folks like me and Mae taking beatings. I guess it looks kind of funny to the kids who make up the World Wrestling Entertainment audience to see these ladies who look like their grandmas getting whacked upside the head and bouncing right back up for more punishment.

What Vince knew was that even at our age—maybe because of our age—Mae and I could provide a special form of entertainment. We could make people laugh, but we could also surprise them with some real wrestling action. Ever since I can remember, those have been two of the main elements to sports-entertainment: comedy

and action. No one ever accused World Wrestling Entertainment of taking itself too seriously, but at the same time fellas and gals in the ring made moves that would cause the crowd to gasp and scream.

We put on a bunch of funny shows. Like at *WrestleMania XVI* in April 2000, when Mae accompanied The Kat (formerly known as Miss Kitty) to the ring to do battle with the "She-Devil" Terri Runnels; the first girl to throw the other out of the ring was to be the winner. The Kat was wearing a fishnet body stocking with a thong underneath and had dyed her hair blond for the match. Terri came in with me by her side, and she had red horns coming out of her head and was dressed in tights.

Now, the story line was that each girl had bribed referee Val Venis by promising him her body. So, to begin with, both girls started trying to kiss the ref, like they were reminding him of the bribe. So don't you know that Mae's got to get her nasty old self into the act, trying to slobber all over that poor man, too. The crowd was whooping it up, because as the match started Mae kept chasing that ref and trying to get her tongue down his throat!

The Kat threw Terri out of the ring, and that should have been the match, but the ref was too distracted dodging Mae's advances. Seeing this, I jumped into the ring, grabbed The Kat, and heaved her over the ropes and out of the ring. Now, of course, the ref saw this and declared Terri the winner! The fans just loved all this mayhem, but The Kat wasn't too happy. She came storming back into the ring, grabbed Terri, and ripped down her tights, exposing her thong for the cheering crowd to see!

But the show that people still come up to me and talk about ran on the TV right around Thanksgiving. When Mae and I got to the arena, Richie, the fella who does all the outfits for Vince, came up to us holding these crazy costumes. "Do you want to wear these?" he asked.

"Did Vince say for us to?" I said.

"No, he said to ask if you would," Richie said.

"Well, put them on us, because if that's what Vince wants, we're doing it," I said.

So Mae got dressed up as a big turkey and I was a Pilgrim. They had us sit in the audience right behind Jerry Lawler, who was announcing that night. Now, Jerry was always giving us a hard time; when Mae got clocked during my match against Ivory, for example, he yelled, "I think Mae Young just wet her Depends!" But we were always getting the last laugh on him, just like we would on this Thanksgiving night.

When Jerry came on the air, we started hooting and hollering behind him, causing him to turn around. Mae was holding her turkey head in one hand—so you could tell it was her—and a flask in the other. She was acting all drunk, taking swigs from the flask, and I was trying to slap it out of her hand. "Mae Young and Moolah!" he said. "What are you two doing back there?"

Mae kept stammering and wobbling, like a drunk. "Sit down!" Jerry said. "You're embarrassing us!"

I kept trying to grab the flask from Mae while the people were laughing. "Don't you two have somewhere to go—like a cemetery!" Jerry cracked.

Well, he tried interviewing us. He said to Mae, "Is it true you gave Stephanie advice for her wedding night? I heard on yours, your husband asked you to take off your pajamas and you weren't wearing any!"

Mae rolled her eyes, took another swig from her flask, and soon enough things got out of hand. A bunch of World Wrestling Entertainment staffers dressed like Pilgrims brought out giant plates of Thanksgiving food, and before you knew it, a full-fledged food fight had broken out. Jerry was right in the middle of it. When his back was turned, I grabbed a big pumpkin pie with whipped cream on it. The fans were egging me on—and so was Mae.

Jerry had his back to me. "Oh, Jerry!" I called, all sweet like.

He started to turn around and I never will forget the look on his face just as I hauled off and let that pie go. It was shock and disbelief and, just before the mushy pie made contact, the beginnings of anger. "You idiot!" he screamed.

"That'll teach you to make fun of your elders!" I said.

Boy, did we get Jerry good that night. But truth be told, some of the most fun during our comeback came off-camera. Like the time after a show in Tampa, Florida, when referee Earl Hebner gave us a lift back to the hotel. At that hotel, you had to take an escalator to where the rooms are, so the three of us were riding up the escalator, with Mae bringing up the rear. Well, Earl and I got to the top and we heard the damnedest noise you've ever heard—I thought the whole escalator had collapsed. I turned around and looked down the escalator, and all I see are Mae's two skinny legs pointing straight up into the air, traveling up the escalator. She had put her suitcase on the escalator in front of her, and it rolled back onto her, knocking her over, and she was pinned underneath it. It was the funniest sight I ever saw, because she was kicking those skinny legs in the air out of frustration, trying to get her luggage off her, and that's all you could see coming up toward us.

"Mae, are you okay?" I called to her, even though I was giggling.

"Yeah, I'm okay, goddammit," she growled.

Come to think of it, Mae was forever falling—inside the ring

and out. One time we were returning a rental car and boarding the shuttle bus to take us to the airport. I got on the bus and then I heard a loud noise behind me; I turned around to see Mae had fallen under the bus. I don't know how she did it, but she went to step up onto the bus, must have missed the step, and slid right underneath us; you could barely see the top of her head poking out.

"What's the matter? What happened?" the bus driver called out, all nervous.

"Oh, it's nothing," I said, laughing. "She's always checking the brakes when we board buses."

Maybe Mae takes so many spills because she likes it so much. I never did meet someone who loved to leave her feet quite so much as crazy old Mae. Maybe her best stunt was during one of the broadcasts, when Bubba Ray Dudley, one of the Dudley Boyz, set out to powerbomb her through a table. He was always doing this to women, but this was a seventy-eight-year-old woman, so Bubba Ray was a little concerned before the show.

Backstage, he came up to Mae and asked if she was sure she wanted to go through with the stunt.

"Honey," she said, "I not only want to be put through that table, I want to be put through that table *hard*."

Bubba Ray didn't disappoint Mae. He powerbombed her through a table set up on the arena floor near the entrance ramp— a ten-foot drop.

Thanks to the way we entertained people, Mae and I found ourselves getting more and more popular. The fans loved us and the media started writing all about us. They called us "divas" and wrote about how Mae was working in a ring in Memphis on the night Pearl Harbor was bombed, and how I held the women's title for twenty-eight years. It was fun to tell people how it used to be in wrestling. Even other wrestlers would just listen to our stories and shake their heads, because they didn't know how tough it used to be.

"I remember people saying 'We're going to get a good payoff,' and you might get twenty dollars," I'd tell them. "That was a good night. I've wrestled for three dollars, a two-out-of-three-falls match, and then I'd come back and do a handicap match."

"We used to wrestle six matches a week, two-out-of-three falls, with an hour time limit," agreed Mae. "The biggest week I had was earning fifty-two dollars."

Some of the young Superstars would approach us backstage and ask how we could still take the bumps we were taking. "Darlin'," I'd say, "if there's one thing I know in this life, it's how to take a bump."

"When we started," Mae would tell them, "if you busted up a knee, you'd soak it in some Epsom salts overnight, tape it up, and get back in the ring. As long as you could use one hand to pull yourself up and down, you did it. So this is nothing unusual for us."

I won't lie to you. It sure was fun to be back in the spotlight

again. And because of Pay-Per-View and cable TV, it was more of a spotlight than I'd ever been in before. Before, I'd travel the country and play to packed houses and have newspaper stories written about me, but millions weren't watching me like they do nowadays on shows like *Raw* and *WrestleMania*. All those years I was champ and I was never as recognized as I was in 1999. All of a sudden I couldn't walk down a street without somebody—often, it was a youngster not old enough to remember when I last was champ—calling out my name.

Whenever we could, Mae and I would talk about how old we were, because we took it serious that we could set a good example for a lot of older people who think time has passed them by. "We'll both be wrestling when we're a hundred," I told one reporter, and the prediction was repeated in every story that came out about us. We started getting mail from people our age, telling us that we were inspiring them. Out of all the fun we had going back on the road, that might have been the best part, knowing that we might be part of the reason some old codger got up off his or her ass and went for a walk or to a senior citizen social event.

The other thing that made our comeback so special was getting to know World Wrestling Entertainment's current group of Superstars. Oh, they were a special bunch, all right. First off, I had known The Rock since he was about two years old. He was born into wrestling, and I had known his father and grandfather. They used to bring The Rock with them when he was just a wee thing, and a cuter kid you just couldn't imagine. Back then, I never thought he'd turn out to be as good or as big as he is, but he is supertalented, and I think that's because he grew up in wrestling. His whole heart and soul is in it, just like mine always was.

Remember how I was talking about how other wrestlers—like Wendi Richter, for instance—got all seduced by the glamour and started to see wrestling as a stepping-stone to becoming a star in

other ways? Well, even though The Rock made two movies and has hosted *Saturday Night Live*, I don't think he'll ever fall out of love with wrestling. In other words, no matter what else he does, The Rock will always be a wrestler, first and foremost. He'll never lose his passion for it because it's in his blood.

Mick Foley is another one who is a wrestler, through and through. He's a wonderful guy with a sweet, beautiful wife and the cutest kids you ever want to meet. And he's a great daddy, too. The thing I love about Mick is that he not only gave his heart and soul to wrestling, but his body, too. He'd show up for shows barely able to walk, but when the lights came up and he put on that costume, it was show time. It's like all the aches and pains went away, for a little while at least, and all he'd care about was entertaining people. I just worry about the long-term effects a lot of the beatings he's taken may have on his body.

Another fella I really like is Kurt Angle. From the time he gets to the ring to the time he leaves the arena, he gives it all he's got. He eats, sleeps, and drinks wrestling. It's his life.

Kurt was a real sweetheart to me. Before a show, I'd be sitting in the dining room where Vince would have laid out a big, impressive spread of food for everybody to eat. I could be sitting at one end of the room and Kurt would walk in at the other end, see me from clear across the room, and shout, "Hi, Mom!"

I'd smile, wave, and yell back, "Hello, son!" And we'd both laugh. We started calling each other "Mom" and "son" one day when we were boarding a flight in Philadelphia. This elderly Jewish guy kept eyeing me up and down in the airport, following me everywhere I went. *Uh-oh*, I thought, *I may have to kick some butt right here in the terminal.*

Well, turns out this fella didn't mean me any harm. He was just a longtime fan. He finally came up to me, introduced himself and his wife, and started talking about how they both had watched me throughout my career. "We've been watching you for thirty years," he said, all excited. "I remember when you were with the Elephant Boy. You haven't changed a bit!"

It was very flattering, but he kept on talking and talking. When they announced that my plane was boarding, wouldn't you know this guy was on the same flight? Just my luck. By the time we were on the plane and looking for our seats, I had me an idea. Kurt was way ahead of us in the cabin, so I said to my new friend, "Wait just a minute. I want you to meet my son."

I got Kurt, figuring I'll let this guy bend "my son's" ear instead of mine while I got settled in my seat. This fella's eyes about bulged out of his head as Kurt approached. He had his wife get his camera, and they insisted on taking photos of me and my son. Kurt shook his hand and the guy started talking to him, and that was my chance to sneak away and get in my seat. Later, Kurt and I laughed

about how I ditched him with my fan, and from then on, he called me Mom and I called him son.

That story shows what's so special about Kurt. He stood there and talked with that fella for a good while. When people ask about him, I always say he's got a good Christian heart. Now, you know by now I'm not one of them God-squad-type people. I ain't out to convert anybody to my way of thinking. What I mean when I say that Kurt has a good Christian heart is very simple: It's just that he conducts himself according to the Golden Rule. He always tries to treat other people the way he'd like to be treated. I try and do the same, even if I'm not always successful at that. But when I see someone like Kurt, who is so young and successful, and he's doing it so well—keeping his head on straight—that inspires me to pay attention to the Golden Rule, too.

Anyway, Vince was right when he first called me about coming back and asked if I was ready to make history. When I beat Ivory for the championship, I made history. Heck, every time I got into the ring at my age, I made history.

I was loving the attention, and like I said, I was loving being an example to people my age. I loved showing them that you don't have to stop living just because you've been around awhile. Which is why I'm not about to give you one of those typical endings to this book. In fact, I'm not giving you an "ending" at all. Too many people my age spend their time thinking about endings. How theirs is going to come soon, how they're powerless to stop it, how their best days are behind them. Bullshit!

If you wake up tomorrow, your best moments are in front of you—if you want them to be. Toward the end of my comeback, I could have given in to the temptation to get all gloomy. See, I started having those dizzy spells. I started blacking out. It was happening in hotel rooms while I was on the road. I knew something was wrong with me, but I didn't want the fun to end. So the only person who knew about my spells was Mae, who tried to get me to see a doctor.

Eventually, as you know, I would see my dear Dr. Tim, who would save my life. But before all that, before I took to calling myself "Dead Woman Walking," Mae and I were drinking some fruit juice in a hotel room, and she was telling me I had no choice but to leave the tour and check into a hospital.

"Mae," I remember saying, "why do you think I've never had one of these blackouts when we're in the ring, entertaining people?"

She shrugged. "Just lucky, I guess," she said.

"It's more than just luck," I said, leaning forward. "Look at yourself. Almost eighty, you get powerbombed through tables. How come you don't hurt yourself? It's because our minds are stronger than anybody knows. I don't pass out because I won't let myself pass out."

We looked hard at each other for a good couple of seconds. "Dammit, you got a point," she said, raising her bottle of fruit juice. "Here's to two of the toughest old broads ever to come down the pike!"

Somewhere down deep, I knew she had a point, too, and that I was going to have to see a doctor, sooner rather than later. But I raised my bottle and clinked hers. "To two old broads," I said, laughing. "We ain't hardly done kicking butt."

EPILOGUE

ALL RIGHT, I BET YOU WERE THINKING I forgot that I've got a secret to share with you. Over the years, I can't tell you how many reporters got frustrated with me because I wouldn't tell them my age. Now don't go thinking that it was some vanity thing. Heck, I always thought I looked darn good for my age, so why should I care if people knew it?

It's just that I was raised to believe that a lady doesn't go around telling people how old she is. It's just not ladylike. And so much of my life has been about doing a manly thing—wrestling—but doing it my way, by staying ladylike. So I never wanted to hand all those people who considered women's wrestling unladylike any ammunition, see? That's why I always dressed so neat and feminine, too. I wanted to prove you could be a lady *and* kick butt in the ring.

But now here I am, sitting on my porch on Moolah Drive. It's a lovely fall day in the year 2001, and I figure that by now, my point about being a lady has already been made. So I reckon it won't hurt anything for you to know that by the time you read this, I will—God willing!—be enjoying the stuffing out of my seventy-ninth (!!) year on this earth.

I'll tell you, darlin', I sit out here, right on the water, with something like 110 geese fluttering around the property, and I shake my head like I can't even believe what a lucky gal I've been.

I'm lucky because I've got the greatest daughter in the world, not to mention my six grandchildren and six great-grandchildren. I'm lucky because they got to see their grandma and great-grandma on the TV, playing the fool. Maybe, just maybe, by watching me, they got the message that anything is possible when you believe in yourself—at any age.

I'm lucky because I had my dear brother Bill for all those years, before God took him. I still miss him so, and think about him every day. I think about how, toward the end, Dr. Tim told him that if he kept on smoking, "Don't come and see me; make your arrangements with Dunbar Funeral Home instead." So cute old Bill, he got himself a brand-new pack of Camel cigarettes and put it in his breast pocket. From then on, when he got the urge to smoke, he'd open that pack and wave it under his nose, closing his eyes, taking in the smell. And then he'd close that pack and put it right back in his pocket, breaking out into a smile that stretched from ear to ear because at least he'd caught a whiff of that tobacco. Now I smile just like he used to, big and wide, when I think about him.

I'm lucky because I've still got friends like Mae, Katie, Daisy, and Donna in my life, friends who saw me survive that brush with death I told you all about. I told God that if He didn't take me then, I'd do what He wanted me to. And that's what I'm trying to do now, trying to appreciate everything and everybody and to remind people that God loves everybody.

It's a lesson I keep reminding my dear brother Chip, who lives on the grounds here with me. Chip is eighty-eight and it's all I can do to keep his spirits up nowadays. He's upset since our youngest brother, Bill, died. Chip is the second to the oldest, and I think he kind of figures he should have gone first. And he's still sad about his wife getting killed. One day they were turning into the Wal-Mart parking lot, when out of nowhere, they were accidentally hit by a car driven by, of all people, their preacher   killing Chip's wife instantly.

So now Chip stays with me here. I built him a little pier about twenty feet out so he can fish. "Sister, I got us enough for a fish fry," he'll say, and we'll fry up his catches and eat 'em while we look out over the still waters.

Just the other day, he said, "Lil, I don't feel good. I can't have much longer here on earth."

"What are you talking about?" I said. "You and me are both going to be playing tennis when we're a hundred years old!"

"You will," he said. "But I won't be here."

THE FABULOUS MOOLAH

"Nonsense," I said. "You've got to move around a little in the fresh air. It'll make you feel better. Let's get in the Caddy and go for a milk shake."

He likes milk shakes. When we got back, he said, "You know what? I feel a little better." Other times, when he seems low, I make him get on my tractor and go across the field with the bush hog. A bush hog is like a big lawn mower that hooks on behind a tractor. So Chip sighs when he hears me say, "It's time to cut the grass, Chip," but I know—firsthand, mind you—how important it is to get out there and do things.

Sometimes, I really have to put my foot down with him. I'll just stand there until he agrees to do something active. "I ain't about to let you quit on me," I'll tell him. And that's what I tell anyone my age. Age is just something you can either give in to—or not.

My doctors have given me a clean bill of health, so I am set to return to the ring. I've been taking some bumps and feel ready to rock-and-roll. But I know one thing. I know I've shown that there ain't no quit in this dog. So rest assured: I'm going to live every last breath out of this life, and I've got one request to make of you. Do old Moolah a favor, sugar.

Do the same.

ACKNOWLEDGMENTS

There are so many people I would like to thank for helping me put my story into words and share the wonderful ride that my life has been for these many years.

First, to my family, including my daughter, Mary Austin, whose support, dedication, and love I just could not do without.

And to my second family, the McMahons: Vincent J., who had the confidence and belief in me that allowed me to succeed; and to Vincent K., Linda, Stephanie, and Shane, whose love and support I treasure dearly.

Much appreciation to my dear friends Katie, Donna, and Mae for all of their love and caring.

To all my friends at World Wrestling Entertainment, especially Stacey Pascarella, who helped make the writing of this book a pleasure.

Of course I must thank all of the fans. It has been a privilege throughout these many years to perform for you, and I certainly thank you for the unwavering support.

And, finally, I would like to thank God for giving me the life that I have led and for bringing me back from the brink of death not once, but twice. I hope that He blesses me with many more happy years to come.

CAPTIONS

PAGE 7: You can never count Moolah out. In 1985, I regained my title from Wendi Richter (and her wacky manager, Cyndi Lauper) when I donned this mask and disguised myself as the Spider Lady.

PAGE 20: Me and Skylo Lowe—a sweet little midget who used to like me to fling him around the ring.

PAGE 34: My first photograph as a professional wrestler (circa 1949).

PAGE 44: My living room in Columbia, South Carolina, has been the site of some top-notch jam sessions. On any given night you might have found me with Jerry Lee Lewis or Hank Williams, strumming my guitar or playing my bass fiddle while crooning sad country songs into the wee hours of the night.

PAGE 58: One-of-a-kind promoter Jack Pfeffer, a classic character in the history of wrestling. Check out those fingernails!

PAGE 61: "I've got you now!" I'm screaming at Jack Pfeffer, after I put him in a Moolah headlock.

PAGE 62: Early on in my career I was known as "Slave Girl Moolah." Didn't mind the name, though, because I didn't care what they called me—as long as they called

me into that squared circle when the bell rang so that I could kick some butt.

PAGE 71: (left) As the Elephant Boy's valet, I spent hours teasing out his kinky hair.

(right) The Elephant Boy was always the perfect gentleman to me outside the ring—which can't always be said for many of the fellas in this business.

PAGE 87: Princess Little Cloud gets a mouthful of Moolah in Dallas, Texas, in the fifties.

PAGE 93: I've had plenty of husbands—too many! But Buddy Lee was my one true love. We sure had us some times.

PAGE 99: A legend is born: On September 18, 1956, J. Marshall Boone of Maryland awards me the $7,500 gold-and-diamond-studded World Championship belt and a bouquet of roses after I outlasted ten girls in an elimination tournament.

PAGE 113: Me and midget Marie Leveaux have some fun on the side of a road during one of our trips.

PAGE 120: My best friend, Daisy Mae, is about to get Moolah-slapped. Don't I look mean? How could such a sweet lady outside the ring have such a mean expression inside it?

PAGE 131: Once I get a handful of hair, it's all over but the shoutin'. Here Judy Grabel is at my mercy. And I didn't show any!

PAGE 136: Judy Grabel gets her revenge with a flying corner scissors.

PAGE 144: I think I pulled more clumps of hair out of Judy Grabel's head than out of any other opponent's. Here she must be thinking about getting a buzz cut before she runs into me again!

PAGE 151: I thought Judy looked like she could use a front-row seat. Notice how the cops do not want to get involved.

PAGE 167: The Spider Lady, aka Moolah, getting back from Wendi Richter what was rightfully mine: the women's championship belt.

PAGE 172: Here I am after wrestling The Lady Angel in 1954. They had to call the cops on me. I started a lot of riots in my day, and I loved it every time all hell would break loose!

PAGE 187: After a tough match, we had drinks at Atlanta's Underground, where the cutest little chimp fell in love with me and wouldn't stop following me around.

PAGE 199: In my gym, the girls watch and learn as I demonstrate a step-over toehold move on Penny Mitchell—the original Spider Lady.

PAGE 201: Another honor came my way in 1991, when *Pro Wrestling Illustrated* awarded me its Lifetime Achievement Award. 'Course, I wasn't done yet.

PAGE 213: There's nothing like friends, and I stay in touch with many throughout the country. Every Christmas their cards go up on my bedroom wall.

PAGE 217: In 1995, I was the first woman inducted into pro wrestling's Hall of Fame. Little did they know then that I'd become champ again four years later!

PAGE 221: Me and my damn midget Katie (known in the ring as Diamond Lil) when we went on a Caribbean cruise in 2000. Katie's been with me for forty years. She calls me "Ma," and I call her "my damn midget."

PAGE 224: I had the championship title for so long—twenty-eight years during one stretch—that I felt like it was a part of me.

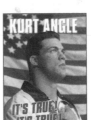